THE COMPLETE BOOK OF STENCILCRAFT

JoAnne Day

With photographs by

Guido Scarato

DOVER PUBLICATIONS, INC., NEW YORK

Published in Canada by General Publishing Company, Ltd., 30 Lesmill Road, Don Mills, Toronto, Ontario.
Published in the United Kingdom by Constable and Company, Ltd., 10 Orange Street, London WC2H 7EG.

This Dover edition, first published in 1987, is an unabridged and slightly corrected republication of the work originally published by Simon and Schuster, New York, in 1974, with the author's name appearing as JoAnne C. Day. The section "About the Author" is an expansion of material that appeared on the dust jacket of the original edition.

Manufactured in the United States of America
Dover Publications, Inc., 31 East 2nd Street, Mineola, N.Y. 11501

Library of Congress Cataloging-in-Publication Data

Day, JoAnne C.
  The complete book of stencilcraft.
  "Unabridged and slightly corrected republication of the work originally published by Simon and Schuster, New York, in 1974"—T.p. verso.
  Includes index.
  1. Stencils and stencil cutting.   I. Title.
TT270.D39   1987   745.7′3   86-29363
ISBN 0-486-25372-4 (pbk.)

To Isabel O'Neil, my teacher,
and the person I most admire

Acknowledgments

I would like to express my sincere gratitude to Iris and Arnold Kronick, Pat Todes, Edie Schneider, and Harriet Ripinsky for allowing me complete freedom in decorating and finishing their furniture, floors, and walls; to Charlotte and Bob Flinn for their trust in my judgment, and to their daughter, Leslie Flinn. Similar thanks go to Irene and Seymour Dunn with a special note of gratitude to Irene Dunn for her ecouragement and unquestioning belief in my abilities. I am especially indebted to Guido Scarato for taking and retaking the photographs needed for this book.

For steering me in the right direction, I thank my agent, Joan Raines, and for making the experience of writing this book a great one, my editor, Julie Houston. Thank you.

About the Author

JOANNE DAY is, first and foremost, a dynamic teacher who is also an expert decorative artist. In 1975 she established the Day Studio in San Francisco after studying, teaching, and earning her journeyman status at the Isabel O'Neil Studio in New York. In addition to lectures and demonstrations, Ms. Day has applied her talents to furniture design, commercial manufacturing, contracting, and design and color consulting, in addition to many private commissions. Her work has appeared in *Architectural Digest*, *The Wall Street Journal*, and other publications. She has authored many books on decorative stenciling and is presently producing video tapes about painted finishes.

CONTENTS

List of Color Plates

FOREWORD

The history of stenciling as a form of artistic expression goes back thousands of years to when stenciling was in common use among the Egyptians and Romans. The Japanese, who have been stenciling for hundreds of years, drew inspiration from the Chinese, and developed it into a precise craft. Many anonymous craftsmen of the Renaissance period were responsible for the beautiful and intricate stenciled decoration seen on the architecture and furnishings of the churches, and it was at this time that the craft was named. The word "stencil" derives from the Old French word *estenceler*, meaning to cover with sparkles; to adorn with bright colors. *Estenceler* is a derivation from the Latin *scintilla*, a spark.

It is likely that American stencilcraft came from Europe. Craftsmen probably found the early Americans eager to have these bright, patterned stencils decorate their homes. Stenciling was applied to walls and floors and furniture. Inspiration for these designs came from field flowers, fruits, patriotic symbols, crewelwork, embroideries, and decorated pottery. The Industrial Revolution put a halt to hand-stenciled decorations, and it is only recently that this unique craft has been revived. Once again stencil work appears in homes across the country, with today's applications more imaginative than ever.

Stenciling can be done by anyone who is interested in the art. The equipment—paper, knife, a stiff brush, and some paint—is accessible to everyone. The advantages are numerous: no particular "creative talent" is prerequisite, preparation of the stencil plate is a simple process, skill in cutting is easily acquired, stenciling can be used for decorating practically any material, and the facility and speed with which ornamentation can be applied delights even the advanced stenciler. Though the procedure is simple, stenciling can be made to turn out highly elaborate and artistic work.

In doing research for this book, it became apparent to me that although books had been written on stenciling, none tried to update the methods and applications and adapt them to today's requirements. My own interest in stenciling began when I was working with interior designers in New York City. I had studied "The Art of the Painted Finish for Furniture and Decoration," taught by a master artist, Isabel O'Neil, and within a very short period of time, I began refinishing furniture for some of New York's most talented designers. I was subsequently introduced to stenciling as an art form and means of decoration. The first piece I stenciled was a round table like the one pictured in color plate 15. I was also amazed to see designers adapting designs for use on floors, walls, furniture, and fabrics with swiftness and ease. It then occurred to me that they were cleverly making use of what is probably the simplest and least expensive reproductive process known.

Shortly thereafter, my good friend and art supplier Louis Horowitz mentioned that a manufacturer of numeral and letter stencils in Jersey City had been, in former times, one of the largest suppliers of design stencils and perhaps had some sitting around a warehouse. I followed up his lead a month later and discovered thousands of stencils ranging from spot designs and borders to giant diaper stencils and multicolor stencils. But more prized than these were the huge catalogs with stenciled records of every design plate made in this country and abroad. The truckload of stencils was delivered to my home. The quantity was staggering. Ultimately they stretched from end to end on the floor of my apartment, while I struggled through the enormous task of cataloging them. Seventy-five years or so sitting in a damp, unheated warehouse made the stencil plates brittle. I experimented and used some of my experience in restoring wood furniture to repair and renew most of the stencil plates. Many of the designs appear in this book.

May I conclude by saying that the satisfaction experienced by using one's own hands to create an artistic work of beauty and individual taste is the ultimate gratification.

ALL ABOUT STENCILING

STENCIL DESIGN

STENCIL TERMS

The oldest recorded stencils were found in China, with the outlines of the designs pricked with a pin rather than cut away. Powdered charcoal was rubbed through the myriad tiny pinpricks and left a stencil impression composed of dots. These dots were connected freehand with lines to form repeated patterns. Cut-out stencils as we know them today appeared with the development of cutting tools and the cheap manufacture of paper.

A stencil design is a large composite of shaped patches of color, which may not relate to each other individually, but together form a decorative design (*Fig. 1*).

A stencil plate is a thin sheet of durable paper on which the stencil design is copied and the various patch areas cut out with a stencil knife (*Fig. 2*).

Stenciling, the process in which a design is reproduced, is done by placing the stencil plate on any prepared surface and applying color through the cut-out openings. A design remains marked out where the coloring matter has reached through the openings of the stencil plate.

An understanding of how a stencil design remains intact after cutting, and does not fall to pieces, is grasped by the following example (*Fig. 3*). If a diamond is drawn on a sheet of paper and its outlines cut with a knife, the body of the diamond is cut away along with the center background of the diamond. When stenciling with this plate, the result is simply a solid diamond of color. Therefore, if a diamond outline is to be obtained, the center piece must be kept in place by joining it to the main body of the plate with narrow bridges or strips of paper known as ties.

Ties are strategically placed to hold the various parts of the stencil plate together and help in the formation of the design. Ties are an integral part of the pattern. The black portions of the stencil designs in this book are cut out and the remaining backgrounds form the ties and stencil plate.

POSITIVE AND NEGATIVE STENCILS

In a positive stencil design, the ornament is stenciled. Most stencils are positive because more techniques can be utilized. Positive stencils can be stenciled in more than one color, shaded and highlighted, and used to decorate any surface (*Fig. 4*).

In a negative stencil design, the ornament is defined by the background being stenciled. The ornament remains the surface color. Negative stenciling is monochromatic (*Fig. 5*).

fig. 1

fig. 2

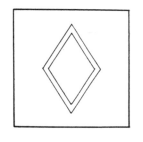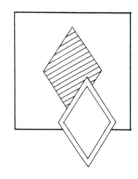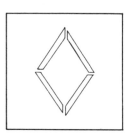

fig. 3

fig. 4

fig. 5

TYPES OF STENCIL DESIGN

Continuous Borders. A continuous border can be a simple geometric or an elaborate floral. These bands of repeating design, as narrow as $\frac{1}{4}$ inch or as wide as 18 inches, are used for the decoration of fabrics, furniture, floors, and walls. All borders can be stenciled in one or more colors (*Fig. 6*).

Fret Borders. A fret is an interlocking, angular band of stencil design that forms a border. The fret is geometric although it may be interrupted by nongeometric design. Fret borders look especially good on floors but can decorate any surface (*Fig. 7*).

fig. 6

fig. 7

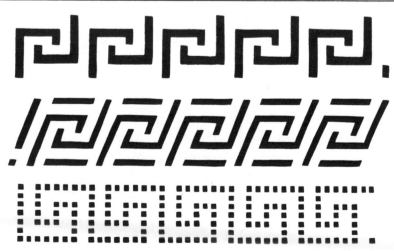

Interrupted Borders. Borders that are interrupted regularly by principal parts differing from the band design are designated interrupted borders (*Fig. 8*).

Spot Stencils. Spots vary in size, shape, and design. Any individual design is considered a spot stencil, such as a flower, a bird, a geometric shape. Spots can be used sparsely or in greater density, and in one or more colors. They adapt to any surface and can be used alone or in combination with borders (*Fig. 9*).

Diaper Stencils. Diaper designs are the most complex stencil designs. The pattern in a diaper continuously repeats itself in all directions. When a diaper is stenciled, the over-all pattern interlocks as if it had no apparent beginning or end (*Fig. 10*).

TERMINATING A BORDER

The best method for terminating a border is a straight line. When you have reached the point at which the border should end, allow a small space and stencil a vertical line. Very narrow borders do not require terminating (*Fig. 11*).

TURNING A CORNER

To continue a border around a turn, a turn-corner stencil can be utilized. The border design is modified slightly to accommodate turning the corner. The turn-corner stencil makes a right-angle turn and flows uninterrupted into the border design. (*Fig. 12*).

A simpler means of turning a border is to use a spot stencil in the corner. The spot stencil is larger than the width of the border. The border is stenciled up to the spot but does not touch it (*Fig. 13*).

A third method is to miter the corner. Mitering is easily understood by observing how a picture frame is joined at corners (*Fig. 14*). Instructions are given in "Stenciling on Floors."

REGISTER MARKS

All stencil designs that run continuously, such as borders, frets, and diapers, must have register marks. Register marks help match up and closely join each setting of the stencil plate, thus keeping the stenciling straight. Register marks are on the right or left side of the stencil plate and repeat part of the design on the opposite side of the stencil plate. For each new setting, the plate is placed to the right or left side of the first impression, with the register mark exactly over its matching place in the previously stenciled impression (*Fig. 15*).

fig. 8

fig. 9

fig. 10

fig. 11

fig. 12

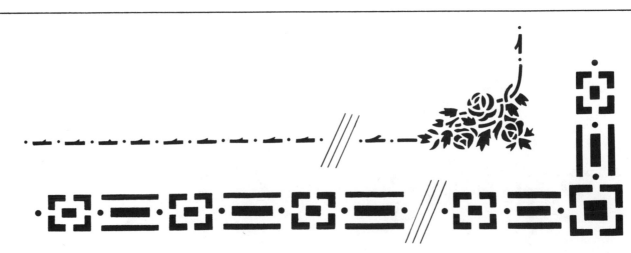

fig. 13

fig. 14

fig. 15

Two-plate stencils require two sets of register marks. Each plate will be stenciled in a different color. The register marks on the first plate are like those described above, but on the second plate the register marks consist of a few cut-out parts from the first stencil plate. After the first color has been stenciled, the second plate is placed on top with the register marks placed over the matching parts of the first stencil. The second color is stenciled excluding the cut-out register marks, which remain the first color. Without these register marks, the exact location of the design on the second plate would be stenciled out of balance with the design on the first plate (*Fig. 16*).

MASKS

Stenciling is often done in more than one color using a single stencil plate. To apply colors using one setting of the stencil plate, the parts to be transferred in the second color are covered with the hand or a piece of masking tape while the first color is transferred. Then, without removing the stencil plate, the second color is stenciled while the first is covered. In this manner the colors are kept clean and separate.

Masks are also used to prevent stenciling beyond a designated limit; for example, one might mask off a diaper stencil before it reaches an enclosing border (*Fig. 17*).

GUIDELINES

Chalk guidelines are applied on fabrics, furniture, floors, and walls to help locate stencil placement. Pencil guidelines are drawn through the center of the stencil plate. Place the stencil plate over the chalk guideline and center the pencil guideline so both are joined and form a single line. Stencil designs run straighter when this procedure is followed. (*Fig. 18*).

ADAPTING YOUR OWN STENCIL DESIGNS

The different stencil designs in this book can be modified and combined to suit your personal taste. Adapting your own stencil designs is simple. Take a stencil design and mask off undesirable portions of the design. You can combine the remainder with similarly modified designs. The result is an original stencil pattern (*Fig. 19*).

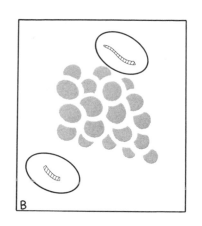

fig. 16

fig. 17

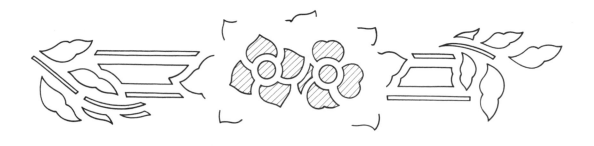

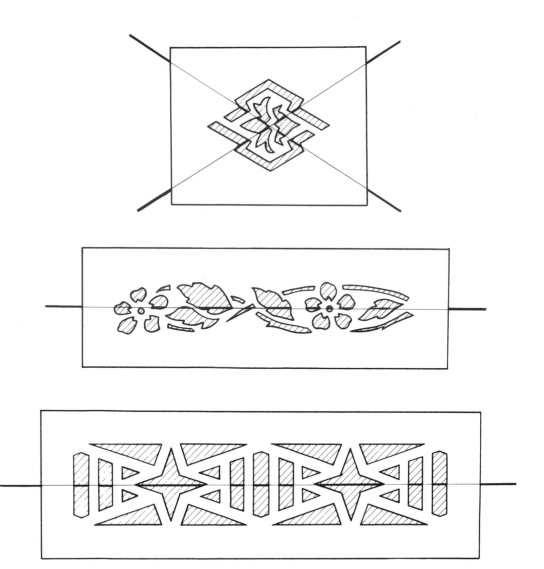

fig. 18

fig. 19

MAKING YOUR OWN STENCIL:

MATERIALS, METHOD, AND TOOLS

Before starting to work, assemble all your tools and materials in one place, preferably on a table that has been protected with a few layers of newspaper.

STENCIL PAPER

Several types of paper can be used for making stencil plates. Your art supplier will have oiled stencil board in stock. This paper is opaque and has been previously waterproofed by treatment with oil. It is a fairly heavy weight and can be used to stencil any surface.

If stencil board is not available, any type of good grade paper can be treated at home for use in stenciling. Manila adapts particularly well. If manila is used, soak a rag in boiled linseed oil and turpentine and wipe it over both sides of the paper until the sheet is saturated. Hang the paper to dry where it will not be damaged or disturbed for twenty-four hours. The more oil in the paper, the easier the knife will cut through it.*

Stencil board, manila and other heavy-duty paper can be protected further by brushing on a coat of shellac or varnish after cutting out plates.

A third candidate, which I frequently use, is heavy-duty wax paper. Sold in sheets, it can be used for tracing because it is translucent, thus eliminating the extra step of transferring a design to a plate with carbon paper. It also cuts easily because of its light weight. However, wax paper is not durable and although a stencil plate of wax paper is quicker to prepare, it should be expected to last for only one job.

TRANSFERRING THE DESIGN

Once the paper is chosen and prepared as necessary, it is ready to receive the design. You will need a good grade of tracing paper, transparent enough to catch every detail of the

---

*Oil-soaked rags are very flammable. They should be submerged in water as soon as you are finished using them.

design you wish to copy. Then you will need carbon or transfer paper for transferring the traced design to the stencil paper. A pencil and ruler complete the tools needed. After the design has been traced from this book, the carbon paper is placed face down on the stencil paper and secured with tape. The traced design is set down on top and taped in its place (*Fig. 20*). With a different color pencil, go over the entire design. In this manner you will have duplicated the design onto the stencil board.

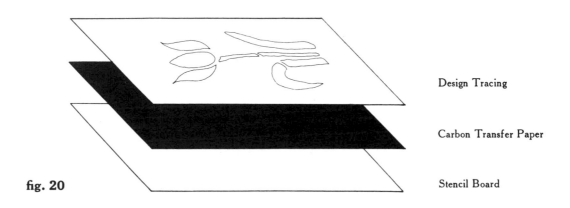

Design Tracing

Carbon Transfer Paper

fig. 20

Stencil Board

ENLARGING OR REDUCING A DESIGN

The designs in this book may not be the proper size for the use you have in mind. If this is the case, you will need to enlarge or shrink the design. The procedure is relatively easy. Take a piece of tracing paper and trace the design. With a ruler, box in the design on four sides. Divide the enclosed area into a grid by placing horizontal and vertical lines at regular intervals. On the stencil board, draw a similar grid that has a corresponding number of squares that will cover the new desired size. It can be longer or shorter for different effects, but the same number of blocks should appear in both drawings. Each block should be regarded separately, and the lines of the traced design that fall in a separate block should be duplicated in the matching block on the stencil board grid. When finished you will have an accurately reduced or enlarged pattern (*Fig. 21*).

CUTTING TOOLS

The Cutting Surface. A piece of plate glass about two feet square with the edges taped to avoid injury serves as the best cutting surface. Your local glass and mirror dealer

fig. 21

or sometimes a large hardware store should have odd-sized remnants for sale at a reasonable cost. Sheet glass, such as windowpanes, should never be used because it will break under the pressure of the knife. Other satisfactory cutting surfaces include marble, Masonite, metal, and hardwood, though a wood surface must be replaced when it becomes heavily scratched. A stack of old newspapers also works well.

Stencil Knives and Blades. Art supply stores usually stock stencil and mat knives. They are generally made of aluminum, and can hold blades that come in a variety of shapes. The aluminum handles are about the length of a pen and as slender as a pencil. The blades come separately, and a fine point usually works best. Both are inexpensive. More elaborate knives for varying purposes can be bought. These include knives with parallel blades for cutting lines, compass knives for cutting circles and arcs, and knives with rotating heads for ease in following a curve. But for the beginner the knife that holds one blade stationary is recommended (*Fig. 22*).

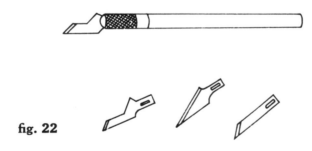

fig. 22

Carborundum Block. A piece of Carborundum should be used for keeping blades sharp. Most hardware or houseware stores carry it for sharpening all knives. Cutting a stencil is so much easier when the knife edge is razor sharp. Your temper as well as your blade will last longer when the Carborundum is used regularly. To sharpen the knife, angle it broadside against the block, put pressure on the blade and swipe it across and back again, just as you would sharpen a kitchen knife.

Circular Punches. These hollow, tubular tools are used to punch holes in leather goods. They can be found in a hobby or handicraft store. It is a piece of metal tubing with one end sharpened to a razor edge. Circular punches come in various diameters, and cut a clean circle wherever the design demands it.

Straight Edge or Ruler. When cutting straight lines, a ruler, preferably metal, should be used as a guide. Place the ruler on the drawn line and run the blade alongside it allowing the ruler to direct the knife.

CUTTING THE STENCIL

Be sure that the cutting surface is clean. Trim the stencil board so that there are margins of no less than one inch and no more than two inches around the transferred design. The plate is always rectangular or square regardless of the form the design takes inside it. The squared corners are used for lining up the stencil plate with the chalk guidelines. Place the stencil board on the cutting surface, but do NOT secure it. The stencil paper must be able to move freely, guided by the fingertips of your free hand, sometimes with the knife working between them. The paper should be able to swing around to accommodate the movement of the knife, rather than have the operator leave his seat to follow the line of design. Hold the knife as you would a pen but slightly more perpendicular. Grasp it firmly but lightly, and use the whole arm for the action, rather than just the fingers. Pull the blade toward you, not away from you (*Fig. 23*). Small details should be cut first. If the large areas are cut first the stencil plate will weaken. Cut all the vertical lines, shift the plate, and cut the horizontal lines that are now in a vertical position. When adjacent lines meet and form a corner or angle, cut slightly past (1/16 inch or less) the ends of the intersecting lines. This prevents ragged or whiskered corners.

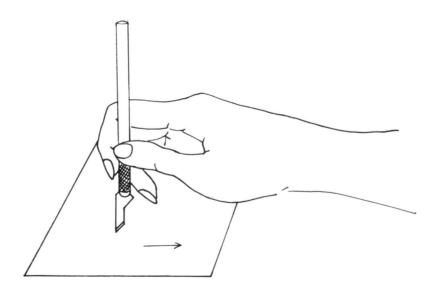

fig. 23

When a tie is accidently cut through, it is repaired with a piece of tape applied to both sides. A jagged line or a ragged corner will stencil exactly that way in every impression of the stencil plate. Accuracy the first time is of absolute importance.

Work with circular punches should be left until last. To prevent damaging the razor edge or breaking the glass by too hard a tap of the hammer, a wood or Masonite cutting surface is substituted. A single tap with a light hammer enables the punch to cut cleanly through the paper.

After you have finished cutting a stencil plate, it is a smart idea to take a stenciled impression of it on another stencil board. This will save you the time and trouble of transferring the design, should the original plate break down and a second have to be cut.

NOTES ON CUTTING A JAPANESE STENCIL PLATE

It is interesting to study a method used by the Japanese for cutting a stencil. The Japanese technique can be adopted for use whenever you do not want ties to interrupt the actual continuity of a design. To look at a Japanese stenciled design, you would marvel at the absence of ties. These stencils look as if the stencil plate would fall apart because portions of the design are suspended in midair and not held together by ties. The method for achieving this effect is ingenious.

A sheet of stencil board is folded in half, forming a double thickness. A regular stencil design is transferred on the upper surface and cut, leaving ties, through the two layers of stencil board. Care is taken to see that the sheets are absolutely flush with each other during the process. The stencil board is opened out when cutting is finished. On either side of the center fold there is a stencil plate exactly similar to that on the other. The inside of the double stencil plate is coated with an adhesive. Fine silk or nylon threads are laid across the tacky plate at regular and close intervals. Human hair is used by the Japanese for this purpose. The threads should form a grid of intersecting lines like graph paper. The sheet is refolded so that the two sides come into uniform contact with the threads between. Pressure is applied until the adhesive has hardened and secured the threads permanently.

At this point the ties that have been holding the stencil together are cut out. If carefully executed, the threads will keep the plate intact (*Fig. 24*). When the coloring matter is dabbed through the plate, the bristles of the brush will work around and underneath the fine supporting threads, producing the uncanny appearance of a stencil without ties.

fig. 24

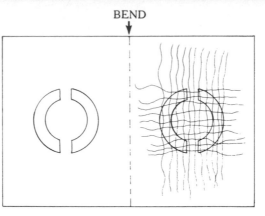

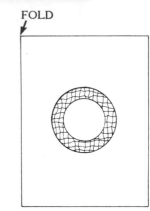

STEP ONE A stencil design with ties is cut through a folded sheet of stencil board and opened out showing duplicate designs on each side

STEP TWO The right side is coated with adhesive and fine threads are laid up and down and across the tacky surface to form a grid

STEP THREE The refolded sheet is pressed together until the adhesive dries, then the ties are carefully cut away

STENCILING TOOLS

Brushes. The brushes used for stenciling come in a variety of sizes. Round in shape, they are composed of three parts; the handle, which is short and stubby, the metal ferrule, which binds the handle to the bristles, and pure hog's bristles of even length with a flat surface of bristle ends. Small stencil brushes are for detail, larger for more open work. They can be used with any coloring matter. It is best to buy good quality brushes as they will give longer service when properly cared for but any new brush will undoubtedly shed some bristles when first used. Shedding can be minimized somewhat by rolling the bristles rapidly between the hands and then knocking the brush lightly against the palm. A brush should be used—clean and dry, the bristles flexible. A trick for drying a freshly cleaned brush is to dip it in a final rinse of denatured alcohol. The alcohol evaporates rapidly and leaves the brush dry and ready for reuse. A stencil brush should receive coloring matter on the flat bottom surface only, never on the sides of the bristles (*Fig. 25*).

Sponges. Any type of sponge can be adapted to stenciling. The best are natural cosmetic sponges. The size of the sponge varies with the area of work. The texture of the fibrous material determines the finished look of the stenciling. They are cleaned the same as brushes. Sponges are always dampened in water before painting.

Newspaper Palette. Newspaper acts as a blotter, absorbing excess color from brush or sponge. Stroking and pouncing the freshly loaded brush or sponge on the newspaper

fig. 25

will get the coloring matter flowing properly. Newspaper also can be used as a test surface before stenciling the actual piece.

Drafting Tape. Tape is used to secure the plate to the work surface. It can be used to temporarily mask off portions of a stencil plate when two or more colors are used. Tape is also used for patching a broken tie. I prefer drafting tape because it is slightly less adhesive and can be removed without damaging the work surface or the stencil plate.

White Blotters. To absorb excess color, a large white blotter is placed underneath fabrics to be stenciled. An art supply store will carry large white desk blotters. Colored blotters are not advisable because of the possibility their color may stain the fabric.

STENCILING MEDIUMS

The coloring matter is properly termed the medium. For stenciling purposes, mediums should be mixed to a fairly thick consistency, somewhere between ketchup and pudding. If the medium becomes lumpy, forms a skin on top, or has foreign particles in it, strain it into another container through a piece of cheesecloth or old nylon stocking.

Japan Paint. Japan paint is flat and oil base. It comes in vivid hues that are lightened by the addition of flat white enamel paint. If a shiny finish is desired add undiluted high gloss varnish. Japan paints have been used for hundreds of years to paint furniture, wood, and to render hand-painted design work. A few drops of japan drier will speed drying times so that one may stencil continuously. Paint thinner acts as the solvent and cleaner. It takes twenty-four hours for japan paint to dry permanently, and any protective varnish coats may be applied thereafter.

Oil Paint. Generally sold in tubes, oil colors are intense. A little goes a long way. Oil colors are thinned with turpentine. Japan drier is added to speed the drying time. Oil colors can be applied in thick solution for opaqueness, or in thin solution for a transparent stained look. Oil color dries with a slightly shiny finish. Oil base enamel deck paint, sold in cans, is best suited for painting floors.

Acrylic Paint. Acrylic colors are water soluble and are the right consistency for stenciling when used directly from the jar. The addition of acrylic polymer varnish, high gloss or mat, will determine whether a finish will dry shiny or flat. Right from the jar, acrylic paints dry with a very satisfactory dull shine. Most acrylic colors stencil opaque but some are marked transparent. The advantage of using water-soluble paints, especially acrylics, is that they dry fast and adapt to almost any surface. Brushes and tools used in acrylic paint are cleaned in water. I use this medium for all surfaces but furniture.

Casein Paint. Also a water-soluble paint, casein tints are more delicate than acrylics. They dry flat and opaque. Casein paint can be used only on surfaces that are going to have a protective coat of varnish. It is most pleasant to work on floors and furniture with this medium.

Stains. Commercial penetrating oil stains can be used to create the look of real inlaid wood and veneer on furniture or wood floors. Stains can only be used on unvarnished, raw wood surfaces. The danger in using stains lies in the thin consistency of the medium. Use a well-pounced-out brush that is nearly dry. There is a tendency for a thin medium to seep under the plate and spoil the work. A wood surface must be coated with a thin coat of shellac. Shellac partially closes the grain of the wood and prevents the stain from bleeding past the outlines of the stencil design. The solvent and cleaning agent is paint thinner. Alcohol and water stains can also be utilized in the same manner but are even thinner and runnier than oil stains, making them even less manageable.

Silk-Screen Ink. The ink made for silk-screen printing, actually an advanced form of stenciling, is well suited for stencil use. It is water-soluble and therefore easy to clean. Used right from the can it has the correct stenciling consistency. Colors can be mixed to any shade or tint desired.

Textile Ink. Also made for silk-screen, these inks are chemically adapted for stenciling on fabrics. They are water-soluble and fast-drying. The heat from ironing causes the ink to react chemically with the fabric, causing the colors to become permanent after this process, giving maximum washability.

Textile Paint. These colors are specially prepared for use on fabrics and come with their own thinner and cleaner. They have an oil base and require twenty-four hours to dry before setting with heat from an iron. I recommend using textile paint on light background material only, as the addition of white textile paint to achieve lighter tints reduces the washability of the fabric. Textile paints can be bought in starter sets at large art supply stores.

Spray Enamel. Spray enamel is sold in vacuum cans. The premixed colors are enamel oil base paint and dry with a glossy finish. They are permanent and washable without added protection after they have dried for twenty-four hours.

Special Spray Kits. Consisting of bottle, sprayer attachment, and compressed air pellet, they can be purchased at hardware stores for use with any medium mixed to correct spraying consistency. Airbrushes can also adapt to any color medium as well as those mediums sold by the manufacturer of the airbrush.

All the mediums listed above lend themselves to stenciling, but it is not to say that other mediums not mentioned couldn't adapt as well. I have even stenciled with latex wall paint. Stencilers in times past used vegetable juices, earth minerals, and soot for their color palette, but now, of course, we have a wide range of mediums and colors from which to choose.

ADDITIONAL MATERIALS

Varnishes. Polyurethane is a high gloss synthetic varnish used for final protective coatings on floors. It is used directly from the can and has no thinner, but brushes can be cleaned in turpentine.

Wood varnish is used as a protective finish on furniture. Avoid buying a cheap grade. Be sure the label reads highly resistant to water, alcohol, heat, and acid, and that the product may be thinned with turpentine. Dilute wood varnish with 40 percent turpentine and heat by setting it in a container of hot water so that it will spread more smoothly and show brush marks less. Wood varnish can be bought in high gloss, satin, or flat finish. Twenty-four hours is the required drying time between coats. Flat wood varnish is not diluted.

Val-oil, a heavy duty varnish, is used for priming metal (as for tôleware) before paint is applied. Val-oil dries in twenty-four hours. If metal is not coated with val-oil, the paint will chip off at the slightest tap.

Japan quick size varnish is a fast-drying synthetic varnish used for laying bronzing powders or metal leaf. Brushes used in japan quick size varnish are cleaned with turpentine.

All varnishes used for protective purposes should be "flowed"—applied with a soft-bristle brush in thin, even coats onto the dust-free, completely dry surface. The heavily loaded brush barely touches the surface as the varnish is applied. Avoid working in damp or humid weather as varnish reacts badly to these conditions. A dust-free atmosphere in a warm room is best.

Shellac. Liquid shellac is sold in 3-, 4-, and 5-pound "cuts" in natural orange or bleached white. I recommend the white 4-pound cut of shellac diluted with 50 percent pure denatured alcohol. A separate white bristle brush may be reserved for use with shellac. Clean the brush with alcohol. Shellac is used for partially sealing raw wood surfaces prior to painting or staining, and between a prepared surface on furniture and stencil design in case of error. Shellac is quick drying, taking less than an hour.

Japan Drier. A quick-drying agent used to accelerate drying and add cohesiveness to an oil base paint. Very little is necessary and the recommended proportion is 1 part drier to 10 parts paint.

Sandpaper. Garnet paper is easily obtained and comes in a variety of weights from rough to extremely fine. Use sandpaper in preparing a wood surface for painting. Use it also between coats of paint and varnish to smooth the finish.

Silicon Carbide Paper. A waterproof abrasive glued to a tough, pliable paper and used for wet-sanding. Referred to in this book as tufback sandpaper, it is black in color and comes in various degrees of abrasiveness. It is used when a particularly smooth finish is desired on paint or varnish.

Chalk, String and Plumb Line. All are used in measuring and transposing guidelines on walls, floors, furniture, and fabrics.

Talcum Powder. Use on hands and stencil plate to absorb moisture and greasiness, preventing possible damage to work surface.

Tac-cloth. A cloth slightly sticky with varnish used to wipe surfaces, leaving them free of dust or any residue from sanding.

Spray Adhesive. Sold in vacuum cans, it is especially useful when stenciling fabrics or any surface that is to be spray stenciled. The side of the stencil plate that is in contact with the surface to be stenciled is sprayed lightly with the adhesive. The plate is then pressed to the surface to assure close contact, and peeled off easily when stenciling is completed.

CLEANING BRUSHES, TOOLS, AND STENCILS

When work is finished, remember the important task of cleaning your tools. The life of your brushes and tools depends largely on the care you take in cleaning them. Proper cleaning will keep color from working up into the bristles near the ferrule. Paint will harden there and destroy the flexibility of the bristles. Excess paint should be squeezed from the bristles between folds of newspaper. If water-soluble paint has been used, wash the brush with brown soap and warm water until the water runs clean. If an oil base paint was used, squeeze the brush out and rinse thoroughly in turpentine. Then wash the brush with brown soap and warm water. When a brush is thoroughly clean, reshape and allow to dry in a position where the wet bristles will not bend. As an added measure, wind a piece of string around the bristles while drying.

If a brush becomes hard, soak it in a special solvent called water-wash until it softens. Then wash it with brown soap and water. Only apply this treatment when absolutely necessary, because the solvent is hard on the brush and expensive to buy.

To clean a stencil plate after using, gently rub with a sponge or rag dipped in the solvent of the color medium.

STENCILING APPLICATIONS

The techniques and methods used for the application of color through a stencil plate are many and various. Several of the following procedures can be combined or used separately to achieve different effects. It is a good idea to experiment with a variety of techniques prior to working on the object you wish to stencil. Not all techniques lend themselves to all surfaces. Color and design are very important in determining a desired effect; but the texture of the stenciling and how it influences the colors and designs is also a major consideration. The effects of boldness, softness, visual illusion (*trompe-l'œil*), age or newness can be achieved with a careful choice of technique. It is well to remember that regardless of method, the crisp, clean outline is of principal importance.

STIPPLING PROCEDURE

Stippling is the most characteristic method used in stenciling. The brushes for this technique are specially designed. Your materials should be gathered together in one location. They consist of color mediums in shallow containers, a palette made of several sheets of newspaper, the stencil plate, and as many brushes as there are colors to be used.

Grasp the brush by the thumb and index finger with the side of the middle finger against the metal ferrule. It is much like grasping a pen for writing, but with the brush held perpendicularly to the work surface. As you become more familiar with this technique you will adjust the grip on the brush to suit your own comfort and needs. I sometimes vary the grip by holding lightly at the end of the handle or make a fist around the handle close to the bristles (*Fig. 26*).

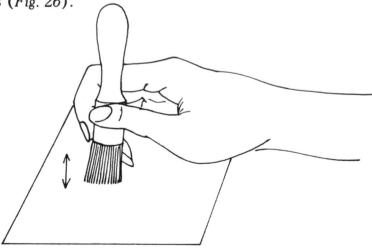

fig. 26

The bristles of the brush must be completely free of any solvents or water used to clean them. Dip only the flat bottom of the bristles into your color medium. The next step is very important. Pounce out the brush by dabbing it perpendicularly on the newspaper palette, which acts as a blotter to absorb excess paint. This action disperses the paint evenly throughout the bristles. It may take a few dips into the paint to get an even coating of medium to show itself on the newspaper. The coating should resemble uniform speckling. Less pouncing will be necessary as the work progresses.

When the stencil plate is in position, secured by tape, and the brush correctly charged with paint, you are ready to begin. The motion of stippling should be rhythmic, with an easy movement of the entire arm. Take care not to tense the muscles in your upper arm or hand. Tensing will cause fatigue and cramps. The perpendicular pouncing is a staccato movement. The primary concern with this method, as with all stenciling, is to be sure your brush is not overloaded with paint. If there is too much paint, it will work its way under the stencil plate and blur the outline. The advantage of the stippling technique is that each stroke of the brush presses the stencil into close contact with the work surface and the perpendicular blow avoids any stretching or twisting of the plate.

The texture of stippling varies with the type of medium used and the pressure you exert. When the pressure is light and the medium somewhat transparent, there will be a slight grain or speckle visible. With increased pressure and a thicker medium the transparency disappears and the speckled grain with it. With a small brush lightly used the speckle is very fine; with a large brush applied with greater force and infused with thinner color the grain will become much coarser and opaque. The blows of the stencil brush should be continuous, overlapping one another until the cut-out portions of the stencil design are completely filled in. The stippling technique is easily executed on any hard surface, such as walls, floors, furniture, and any fabric without pile or a raised nap.

Color blending—the intermingling of two or more colors—is easily done with stippling. Using one stencil plate, the colors are applied consecutively and actually intermingle, forming areas of a third color. Successful blending is achieved when the first color applied is slightly thicker and wetter than the second color, and does not fill in the entire design. By immediately stippling with the second color, over the still wet surface of the first, the remaining ground fills in and the colors intermingle. On a leaf design the effect would be a dark green (first color 70 percent coverage) at the outer edges with a lighter green (second color 30 percent coverage) toward the center and a mottling of the two colors apparent throughout. Blending is most beautiful when the colors are analogous in character.

SPONGING PROCEDURE

Sponging seems to be the next most widely used method for stenciling. The sponge itself determines, to a large degree, the texture of the finished work. Natural cosmetic sponges, irregular in shape, can be purchased at almost any drugstore. Manufactured sponges used for household chores are adaptable. Foam rubber can also be utilized. The porous qualities of sponges differ and will effect distinct textures. I work with sponges small enough to fit in the palm of my hand. Bigger sponges can be used for large flat area work. Sponges can be easily cut to fill any requirement.

Gather your materials in one location before starting. Use one sponge for every color. Grasp the sponge lightly with your fingertips. Care should be taken to see that the pressure on the sponge is light because squeezing and pressing will cause the medium to run out of the sponge (*Fig. 27*).

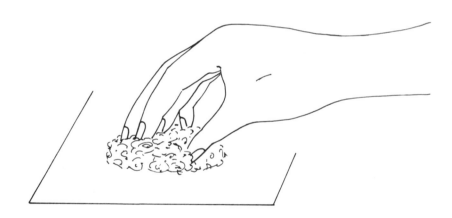

fig. 27

With this method there is no way to avoid getting paint on your hands. When using oil base paints, I recommend the use of a commercial protective coating often referred to as "the invisible glove." The white cream is rubbed on and disappears. It protects the hands and makes cleaning them a simple matter. It can be purchased in any hardware–paint store. Latex or acrylics present no cleaning problems. As for rubber gloves, surgical or otherwise, I feel strongly that they interfere with the delicate sense of touch.

Dip the sponge in the color medium prepared to a much thinner consistency. Squeeze to remove the excess liquid and to disperse the medium evenly throughout the sponge. Use a newspaper palette for absorbing and testing the color. The action of dabbing and pouncing is never forceful: it is quick but somewhat timid. Dabbing, rubbing, and wiping can be used separately or in combinations. The effect of sponging is more dappled than speckled.

Since this technique works well with transparent colors for glazed effects, it lends itself well to shading. Shading is obtained by the use of transparent glazes or washes over flat, opaque stencil designs. These glazes darken the original stenciled color, creating shadows and the illusion of three dimensions. For instance, on a dark mahogany stained tabletop, a shell design stenciled on in a pale sand color is allowed to dry. A thin color solution of burnt orange is sponged on top of the design through the same stencil plate. The burnt orange glaze can cover partially or totally the previously stenciled areas. This will give the effect of aging and antiquing the seashell design and soften the look of two divergent colors (dark mahogany and pale sand). It will add depth and dimension to the shells at the same time.

A glaze can be used to change or modify any color. A wash of blue over yellow will produce green, a wash of deep green over pale blue will produce turquoise. Color blending is also possible with sponges (see chapter on Stenciling on Walls for detailed procedure, page 89). This method of application is adaptable to hard surfaces, such as floors, walls, and furniture. It can be used for fabrics, but other techniques are more successful.

BRUSHING PROCEDURE

This technique is more difficult to manage. An ordinary paint brush with fairly stiff bristles is used. The brush should be about an inch wide and the bristles two inches or so in length. To succeed with this method you must use a sturdy stencil plate made of strong paper which cannot be easily pulled out of shape. Good contact between the stencil plate and work surface is absolutely necessary to overcome the natural tendency of the brush to sweep the color under the stencil plate. Contact is accomplished by coating the back of the plate with a commercial spray adhesive made especially for temporary mounting. If directions given on the can are followed, it is possible to achieve complete contact between surface and stencil plate. When the plate is being removed after stenciling, great caution must be taken not to rip any delicate ties in the design. Ripping can be minimized if the adhesive is applied sparingly or if the newly sprayed adhesive is blotted with a soft lint-free cloth to dull the adhesion.

Mix paint or medium to a consistency of heavy paste. When the stencil plate is in place, dip the brush into the paint halfway up the bristles. Scrape the excess off on the side of the paint container. Run the charged brush back and forth across the newspaper palette to disperse the paint throughout the bristles.

Begin the first stroke with the tip of the brush in the center of the cut-out design. Proceed to the outer edge of the design leaving a slight deposit of paint there. Work with even strokes in this manner until the entire design is filled in. The streakiness of the brush strokes should be apparent. The dark line of more solid color showing at the edge suggests an intaglio or sunken effect. In Italy, during the eighteenth century, Venetian period furnishings imitated the elaborate wood carvings of low relief by incising a gesso surface. The slight groove cut into the gesso surface was tinted with darker color for emphasis, and although the surface remained smooth and flat with no relief, a design outlined in this manner appeared three dimensional. Brush stenciling uses the same principles to achieve the intaglio effect of incised carving or inlay work (color plate 2). This procedure is particularly rich and striking when used in transparent color or stains on new wood surfaces, suggesting, but not exactly imitating, inlaid woodwork or marquetry.

The brushing method is best suited for those surfaces that intaglio itself would adapt to, wood furniture and walls. The look is distinctly different from stippling or sponging and is well worth a little practice to master. Color blending or shading is superfluous as it would be redundant.

SPRAYING PROCEDURE

Spray work is the least arduous of all stenciling procedures. The pressure-sealed can of paint requires no mixing, almost no physical strain to apply, and no cleaning of materials when through. Of course you have less to say about the colors since they are determined by the manufacturer.

When you use commercially manufactured spray paints, wear a face mask. Work in a well-ventilated room. The fumes can be overpowering.

Spraying produces a texture similar to but much finer than stippling. The delicacy possible with this method is one of its chief recommendations. For example, colors can be graded or blended; one tint can be superimposed over another without waiting for the first to dry. Spray work is especially valuable when working on fabrics because it does not interfere with the weave. Fabrics with a nap or pile, such as velvet or mohair, remain erect instead of being matted and laid flat.

The procedure for spraying is very simple. Begin by protecting any surrounding area with newspaper or tarpaulin, since the finely divided color blown onto the prepared surface by a current of pressurized air will leave a slight residue over everything within a radius of three feet. The residue can be quite disconcerting when a spray color contrasts with the background. Commercially manufactured spray paints are almost always permanent enamels and extremely hard to remove. The same thing applies when using a commercial fabric spray.

A spray paint should be tested on newspaper to make sure the cap is not faulty. Shake the can, then spray one very light, even coat. If the paint starts to sputter from the can it is usually due to uneven finger pressure on the cap. Let dry two or three minutes and spray again. When you become more familiar with this technique and the variations achieved from different pressures and distances, you will be able to execute most stenciling with one coat. If you spray too heavily you risk letting the medium run behind the stencil plate, especially on a vertical wall. On all surfaces, it is a good idea to use the spray adhesive on the back of the stencil plate, pressing it flat against the surface, to prevent paint from seeping behind.

When removing a stencil plate, be particularly careful not to smear the paint. Spray enamel is sticky and slow to dry. For this reason, when overlapping stencils, as in a continuous border design, note if the paint is still tacky. Once the plate is removed, it cannot be replaced until the paint surface is completely dry.

Color blending by spraying differs in that the separate colors actually mix. However, a fine delicate spray of paint particles falls on the prepared surface and lets tiny specks of the background show through, and depending on the amount of paint sprayed, the surface will appear shaded. When different colors are sprayed, one on top of another, the fine particles overlap. Because they are so close together you have the illusion of color change. Therefore, a spray of pink on top of a spray of blue will give a purplish–violet color. A combination of red over yellow will become orange. Always spray from the lighter color to the darker. If done in the reverse, the dark color tends to swallow up the paler tint placed on top and produces muddy shades. A faint spray of the earth color brown will add depth and perspective to any color it is used to shade.

The possibilities are endless, and the subtle differences in color are lovely. Color blending can be achieved in all the methods described in this chapter but none more successfully than in spray work. If the color is applied delicately, spraying can be used to shade and tint over a surface previously stenciled by another method. All surfaces adapt well to this procedure.

Highlights and Shading . . . Mastering a Concept

Highlights and shading are effects that require some experimentation to master. They are used in combination with the previously described methods to give more dimension to the overall tone of a stencil design. To use them successfully, first you must understand what they are and how to place them correctly in a design.

A highlight can be defined as the point at which the most light is reflected off a represented form. Shading is defined as the introduction of degrees of darkness in order to render light and shadow on a stenciled design.

The placement of highlights and shadows requires some thought and imagination, and the procedure described here is a simple introduction to a concept utilized not only in stenciling but in all phases of art. On a practice board prepared with a painted surface, stencil a design. Remove the stencil plate, imagine that the design is slightly raised. Make a mental image of the sun (or light source) coming from the upper right-hand corner. As the rays of light shine across the design, the edges closest to the light source will reflect the most light and those areas most distant will be cast in shadow.

The light source does not always have to be placed at the upper right-hand corner. If one has a rectangular room with a set of windows on one wall, the light from the windows will be considered the source. As the stenciled designs on the adjacent walls get farther and farther from the windows, the shadows will deepen and the highlights fade. The highlighted edge will be the edge nearest the light and the shaded edge the farthest away. In the case of direct lighting, as on the wall facing the windows, highlights would appear top and center in the design with shading on right and left sides and bottom. Overhead lighting would produce the same effect as direct lighting. But in the case of a movable object such as a piece of furniture, fabric, etcetera, the imaginary sun in the upper right-hand corner is best (*Figs 28* and *29*).

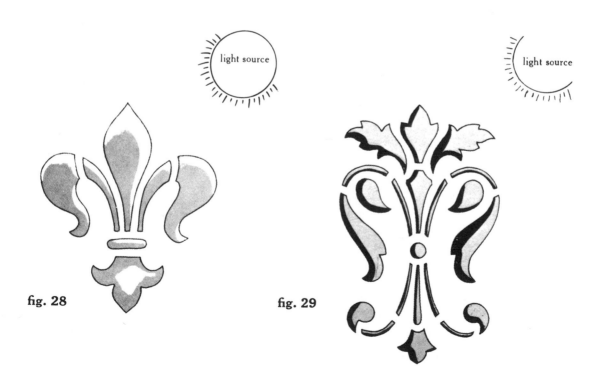

fig. 28   fig. 29

For further clarity, take a shiny red apple or other glossy-surfaced object and place it near a real light. Walk around it and study the effects of the light upon it. The varying degrees of light and dark should be obvious. When we create the mental image of our stencil design in three dimensions, the stencil becomes capable of reflecting light in the same way as the apple. At the points of intense light and dark, highlights and shades are rendered to create an illusion of three-dimensionality. Elaborate florals can take on the naturalistic look of the flowers they are imitating. Simple, flat geometrics can give an appearance of richness and depth.

When this concept is understood, highlighting and shading can be effected simultaneously with the stenciling technique you are employing. I have described all the procedures in this chapter in order to help the stenciler achieve any desired effect and to show the variety of techniques needed to do so. Ultimately, however, it is best to keep in mind that a stencil design is most effective when done simply. When a specially rich effect is desired, as in ornate work, several methods of stenciling may be combined as long as a purely decorative effect is intended. Any effort to create a hand-painted effect with stencils will simply defeat the candid imitation of design that stenciling is and should be.

HIGHLIGHTING

For our purposes, a whole stencil design is the represented form and the highlight area is the lightest color in the design. Highlighting a given area is accomplished by removing some or most of the color that has been stenciled. The original background surface—on which the stencil has been painted—must be lighter in shade than the stencil itself. For example, on an off-white wall, a pattern of leaves and foliage is stenciled in a forest green. When some of the green is removed by rubbing or wiping, it reveals traces of the white wall tinted to varying degrees with the green residue. These light spots are the highlights. Highlights can also be rendered by the addition of lighter color. On the same dark green foliage design, a lighter shade of the same green is stenciled in determined areas by stippling, sponging or spraying. The same light spots result. Highlighting is thus achieved even when the original background surface is darker than the stencil.

SHADING

In stencil work, shading surrounds a highlight. It always appears at the outer edges of the design. Shading is done by covering areas of a painted stencil design with a thin transparent color in order to modify the original tone and darken it. In fact, when shading is done correctly, it creates highlights by emphasizing the lighter, unshaded areas.

In stenciling, one should not strive to duplicate hand-painted work—stencil techniques are meant to save time and effort while achieving distinctive results.

The following five procedures are used specifically for highlighting and shading, but only to embellish the basic procedures of stippling, sponging, brushing, or spraying.

WIPE-OUT PROCEDURE

Wipe-out stenciling can be employed as a method to highlight and shade freshly painted stencil work when the stencil plate is still in place. Effects are somewhat similar to those created by the brushing procedure. The process is one of removing color with a soft cloth, called a wipe-out rag, in order to expose the background color. After a design has been stenciled by stippling or sponging, the inside section is wiped out, leaving the inside lighter in tone than the extremities.

The rag should be soft and absorbent, with little or no texture in the weave. I make rags from soft cotton T-shirts and underwear after they have worn out. Cheesecloth that has been washed and dried to remove the sizing is also very effective. Use a rag no larger than 6 inches square. Depending on the amount of wiping to be done and the number of colors in use, you will need to cut a number of squares to meet your requirements. Sometimes a soft pliable sponge can be utilized for wiping—the procedure is the same.

Immerse the rag or sponge in the same solvent used with the paint medium—i.e., if the design was stenciled using water paint, the solvent is water; using oil base paint, the solvent is turpentine—wring out thoroughly, and twist it in a dry piece of terry toweling. The wipe-out rag should be just barely damp, and can even be used dry if preferred. Too much solvent on the rag will wipe out all the color and smear paint behind the stencil plate.

Fold the damp square of fabric and wrap it around the index finger. The freshly painted design can be wet to surface-dry. Determine the highlight areas and, with the wrapped index finger, proceed to wipe color out. Allow the light-colored ground to show through the most at the points on the design that reflect the most light from your imaginary light source. Here again is the risk of wiping the color under the stencil plate.

The texture achieved by wiping can be primitive and streaky, or subtle and perfectly blended. With discreet use of the wipe-out rag, interesting effects can be achieved, but it is easy to overdo it and destroy a good design.

STAINED GLASS AND WIPE-OUT EFFECTS

A more elaborate procedure for wipe-out stenciling is used to create a stained glass effect. Used for wall panels or painted on a canvas to be stretched, framed, and hung, as illustrated in color plate 22, the effect is unique. Instructions can be divided into one-color or multicolor work.

Choose a stencil that has ties as the outlines of the design. The most suitable subjects for this type of work are human figures, florals, or geometric combinations that form an abstract design. Look for designs that you can use for original stencils—visit antique shops where authentic stained glass panels for cabinets, doors, and windows can give you ideas. The beautiful, fluid designs of art nouveau are well adapted to stained glass and thus to stencil. Church windows are another source for ideas, with stained glass figures and symbolic designs. Tiffany lamps, often with quite elaborate designs, are also an interesting source for stencil patterns.

Once you have found a design in stained glass, you must reproduce it on stencil board. Using a broad charcoal, draw in the stained glass leads; the width of the charcoal is the width of the tie. The masses inside the ties represent the pieces of stained glass—and the cut-out areas of your stencil—and will vary in size and shape. The broad charcoal lines should connect to one another like a maze. You will be able to follow a line from one location in the finished design to any other location without lifting your finger from the plate. After you have transposed the design completely, make a last-minute check that the ties are wide enough to be strong when the masses are cut out. Spray the charcoal design with fixative and cut out the masses inside the charcoal lines with a razor or mat knife, using the rough charcoal edges as your guidelines. The stencil is ready for use when you finish.

A large stained glass design should be first thought of as a wall hanging, either stenciled directly on a wall or on canvas. The surface upon which the stencil will be applied must be prepared. Clean and paint it a light color or white. Measure the size of the design, adding ½ inch to each side for a border (it can be wider if preferred). Place pieces of tape on the wall to form an enclosure of the established dimensions. If you are stenciling on canvas, stretch it out on a floor that is protected with a thick stack of newspaper and secure with tacks or pushpins. Measure and tape in the same manner as for the wall. The raw linen or cotton duck is painted with two coats of acrylic polymer gesso and allowed to dry. Drying time should be less than an hour or until a hand can be brushed across the surface and not pick up any residue.

A stained glass stencil can be one color only or several. In one-color work, the background is tinted with a light color of your choice. Remember that it is the color that will be exposed when wiping is completed. It is a good idea to use oil mediums for this technique. Hard rubbing on a water-base surface is apt to mix the original light ground with the applied dark ground. The result will be muddy. Oils, of course, require a longer drying time between steps, at least twenty-four hours. Water paints can be used with isolating coats of white shellac between steps.

There is one more step before stenciling—painting what will eventually form the ties.

Mix a charcoal gray–to–black oil color to a thin, watery brushing consistency. It should be thick enough to give an opaque covering with one coat, and thin enough to wipe off easily. Paint the entire enclosed space where your design will be with this medium, taking care that brush strokes are all in the same general direction. When this dark ground is still wet, you are ready to proceed.

Attach the stencil to the freshly painted surface with tape, making sure the tape is not placed on the semiwet area as it will most likely peel off. With the wipe-out rag ever so slightly dampened with turpentine and wrapped around the index finger, wipe out the dark color through the openings in the stencil plate. You can reveal as much of the background tint as necessary to suggest highlights, shading, and desired tone. When the plate is removed, the ties will have remained the darkest part of the finished work, as with stained glass leads. The dark coat is applied with ease and wiping out is done rapidly.

In multicolor work, actual stenciling is required. On the prepared background surface, the plate is attached and the various colors are stenciled by stippling or sponging. Use masks to prevent colors from overlapping each other on a single stencil plate. When all the colors have been applied and the plate removed, only the ties will show in the background color. Let the stenciling dry for twenty-four hours, and then paint over it with a dark ground color, over the entire surface, and proceed wiping out as for the one-color treatment above.

The charm of this type of wipe-out stenciling is in the variety of tone and the blurred edges that result from a little effort on the part of the stenciler. When the finished wall or canvas has dried for several days nothing further is required. However, a mat fixative or varnish can be applied to the canvas or wall as is done with good paintings.

SPATTER PROCEDURE

Spatter work has a peculiar quality of its own that is worth using occasionally, but it is too slow for general use. The texture produced from spattering is very similar to spraying and more easily controlled.

Any stiff-bristle paintbrush will do. Cut the bristles evenly with a razor to a length of 1 inch. You can also use a stiff-bristled toothbrush. The consistency of the medium used should be thin and watery. Spoon the medium onto a piece of wax paper, which is used as a palette. Dip the end of the brush into the medium and pounce it out on the wax paper before application. Aim the brush toward the area to be stenciled. Pull the bristles aside with the right index finger and allow them to spring back, so that they throw off the color in tiny blobs and specks, slightly coarser and more irregular than a spray. The brush should be aimed at the area to be spattered. The slower the movement of the index finger across the bristles the finer the spatter. As you work, wipe the medium off the index finger occasionally during the spatter process, since accumulated paint can otherwise drip unexpectedly and fall on the work surface (*Fig. 30*).

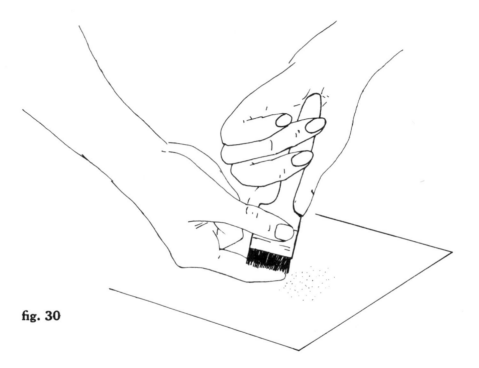

fig. 30

To soften the effect created by spatters, a soft rag is blotted lightly over the still somewhat wet specks of paint, blurring the edges ever so slightly, and creating a delicate highlight or shade. The area around which you are working should be masked to prevent stray spatters falling where not directed.

Spattering is employed for shading and highlighting prominent points in the design after they have been stenciled by other means. As an example: a geometric border interrupted regularly with a large floral rose. The geometric portion of the design is stenciled in a flat gray–green. The rose is stenciled in a pale mauve. Specks of a deep burgundy are spattered and blotted from the center to the outer petals. The spattering should be more concentrated in the center with a very few specks reaching the outward fringe of petals. This intensifies the depth of the rose, with the speckles acting as a kind of color shading. It also gives a hint of perspective.

PASTIGLIA RELIEF PROCEDURE

Pastiglia is the formal name given to raised relief work or carving. The Orientals are masters at this form of decoration. Chinoiserie rendered on lacquer furniture projects the figures from the surface, detailing every fold in a garment, every feather on a bird. The raised elements were built up with coat after coat of gesso, then gilded and burnished to great brilliance. Eighteenth-century Venetian furniture adopted this technique to replace costly wood carving, but it quickly evolved into a separate art. Pastiglia can be considered the reverse of intaglio or incised design but they both produce the same three-dimensional effect.

Relief work in stenciling is at best a very primitive form of pastiglia. The finished work projects only slightly from the background surface, but since this produces an ornate effect in itself, the procedure should be confined to simple patterns of classic design, such as Greek keys, frets, or fleur-de-lis. The design is cast or molded on the surface by filling a deep-cut, thick stencil plate with plaster composition (color plate 1).

Walls are the only practical surface for the application of relief work. The wall surface should be clean, unsealed plaster because it is the most highly absorbent and will allow the wall surface and the plaster composition to bond with each other. If this is not possible, the painted wall must be roughened with sandpaper where the design will be applied to give it a slight tooth to hold the relief work. The roughened area is then given a thin coat of diluted white glue and allowed to dry. Upon completion of the relief, the entire wall is painted.

For relief, the material used for the stencil plates must be ⅛ to ⅜ inch thick. Soft wood veneer, cork or linoleum work very well. Transfer the design to the plate surface and cut it out with a jigsaw. Bevel the cut edge so when the plate is placed flush against the wall the angle slopes inward toward the surface to be stenciled. The plaster composition is forced into and under the slanted edge. With the bevel slanted inward, the stencil plate will come off the wall without breaking the edges of the relief (*Fig. 31*). If the material

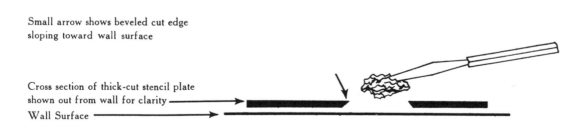

Small arrow shows beveled cut edge
sloping toward wall surface

Cross section of thick-cut stencil plate
shown out from wall for clarity ————

Wall Surface ————

fig. 31

used for the plate is not waterproof it must be made so by varnishing prior to use. Prepare the plaster composition from dry patching plaster, white glue and water. Sift the patching plaster and mix with enough water and white glue to make a stiff putty.

Hold the stencil plate firmly against the wall and force the mixture into it with a putty knife, spatula, or trowel. The surface can be smoothed or roughened to resemble stucco. The plate must be held in place for a few minutes with each setting to give the plaster a chance to set. The plate is then lifted smartly from the wall surface so as not to harm the edge. The fresh dry plaster must first be given a coat of shellac to seal it and stop absorption. If the shellac is neglected the plaster will absorb the liquid in whatever color medium chosen, resulting in splotchy, powdery color that will continue to fade with time. After the relief work has set twenty-four hours it can be painted.

Relief stenciling is listed here for craftsmen and real enthusiasts of stencil work. Relief can be utilized by a beginner who wants to highlight points in a more elaborate stencil design, such as the center of a flower, the eyes of an animal, or a small component of a geometric design. The depth of design causes it to cast a slight shadow and show perspective. In relief, I prefer white on white or the same color for both background and design. The subtle relief lends elegance to any decor. When contrasting colors are used, the relief is wasted since color, and not dimension, immediately becomes the focal point.

BRONZE POWDERING PROCEDURE

The result of bronze powdering is different from all other effects mentioned in this chapter as the medium is metallic in nature. The glint of gold, silver, copper, or bronze embellishes a design. Powders are used to imitate the look of real gold and silver leaf. Occasionally, for a specific look, entire designs can be stenciled in bronzing powders alone. But most often powders are used to highlight other techniques. The powders can be bought in any hardware–paint store. They come in a rainbow of metallic colors as well as the traditional golds and silvers. They should be used discreetly for they *are* instantly eyecatching. Anything overdone can result in a garish display of bad taste. The powders consist of various alloys, essentially copper and tin, or copper and zinc. The silver powders are made from aluminum. There are a number of ways to stencil with powders, the most time-consuming producing the most perfect results. But for the usually tiny highlight points to be powdered, the extra time is worth spending.

The first method of powdering is for small highlight areas and should be done only when the weather is clear and dry, rather than rainy and humid, since varnish will be used and its drying ability is greatly hindered in a damp or moist atmosphere. The varnish is called "Japan gold quick size" and is carried in most paint and art supply stores. When slightly tinted with color, it becomes a stencil medium ready for use. The addition of an oil color tint is necessary because quick size by itself is transparent. This method of powdering will produce the most satisfactory results and the closest imitation of the luster of real gold and silver leaf.

First dust some talcum powder over the surface to receive the stenciling. Stippling (page 33) is the best method for stenciling quick size. Dip the brush into the medium and thoroughly pounce out on newspaper. Only the slightest amount of size is needed. The brush is worked almost dry. Put stencil plate in place and stencil the design onto the surface by stippling. The size will come to tack anywhere from ten to forty-five minutes. You must check often to see whether the sized surface has dried to the correct tackiness. When a finger touched quickly to the surface feels a slight adhesion, but does not leave a fingerprint, it is ready. Do not worry about fingerprints, in any case, since they will be covered. If powders are applied to a surface that is still wet they will dull, on an overdry surface they won't adhere. From the time the size reaches the correct tack, you have five minutes or so to apply the powders before it becomes too dry.

The bronzing powders are applied with a homemade tool called a velvet bob. Take a 6-inch square of deep pile velvet and lay it wrong side up on a table. Place a ball of cotton the size of a walnut in the center on the underside and pick up the sides and corners of the velvet. Stretch a rubber band around the cotton, isolating it and forming a velvet-covered balloon. Grasp the bob at the rubber band just as if it were a brush. Dip the bob into the powders and tap the excess off with the index finger. The bob is then rubbed, stroked, and wiped over the tacky surface in a circular direction (*Fig. 32*). The stencil

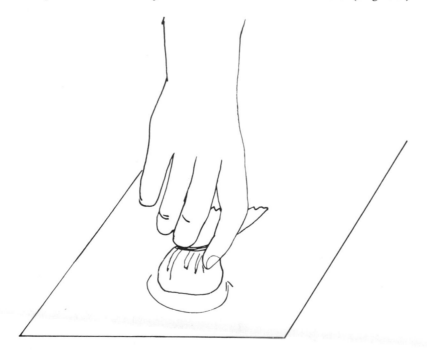

fig. 32

plate must be in place prior to commencing, since the powders are so fine they will ingrain themselves everywhere, including into the pores of the unprotected background paint. Let the powdered surface dry for twenty-four hours and protect the finished work with a coat of clear, high gloss varnish. This is a necessary finishing procedure for all powdered surfaces regardless of method because it stops the oxidizing action that makes the metal become tarnished and dull.

For larger areas being stenciled in bronzing powders, a second, faster method is to mix powders into a clear medium and stencil directly on the surface. The clear mediums that can be used are quick size varnish for oil base work, acrylic gloss polymer for water base, bronzing liquid, which is a lacquer base, or even shellac, which is an alcohol base. All are quick drying. The mixture is 1 part powder(s) to 4 parts clear medium. It is stippled onto the surface, allowed to dry twenty-four hours, and protected with clear, high gloss varnish. This method of stenciling can inexpensively reproduce the effect of the most beautiful metallic wallpapers.

Another interesting effect can be obtained by the use of a transparent color glaze over gold or silver. The effect is like jewel enamel (color plate 3). The glaze is mixed with a high gloss varnish base and a touch of color. For oil glazes, japan quick size is used, for water color glazes, acrylic gloss polymer. Over silver or aluminum powders, use a cobalt blue glaze; on copper or gold, a glaze of medium chrome green or vermilion is best suited.

GILDING WITH LEAF

I would like to briefly mention gilding with leaf, which has a more brilliant effect than powder. Although gilding with the fragile sheets of real gold and silver leaf should be left to more experienced artisans, there is an imitation leaf on the market that is easy to work with: aluminum leaf for silver and dutch metal leaf for gold. If the hands are rubbed with talcum powder to remove all moisture, the leaf can be carefully picked up and placed against a sized surface that has come to tack. Use a piece of velvet to gently rub the leaf and remove the excess. A much higher brilliance is obtained with leaf than with powders, but more patience is required. Leafed surfaces must also be protected with high gloss varnish.

AIRBRUSH PROCEDURE

I will mention airbrush stenciling only briefly. The textural effect has been more thoroughly explained under spraying, but you can achieve much more subtle color tones for shading and highlighting with an airbrush. The use of an airbrush for stenciling can be likened to a magic wand. The airbrush is a compact tool that comes with its own compressor to maintain air pressure. A little larger than a pen in size, it can produce anything from the faintest hairline to solid color.

Almost any liquid medium can be adapted for use with an airbrush. Prepare the medium according to the manufacturer's instructions and pour it into the cup attached to the airbrush until half-full. A 20-pound pressure is usually satisfactory for a fine spray; a reduced pressure will effect stippling and spattering. If the airbrush starts to sputter, the medium is too thick. Using a relaxed arm and wrist motion, test out the loaded brush on paper. Slight finger pressure releases the spray. Colors can be blended and deepened with successive coats when the previous coat has dried. Finished work should dry twenty-four hours. This method adapts itself to any surface, horizontal or vertical, fabric or wood.

One curious effect of the spraying processes is that when a stiff stencil plate is used, the plate can be held a little distance from the work surface, a half inch to an inch. The stenciled design is reproduced with a soft cloudy outline instead of the crisp, clear outline given by contact. This type of treatment is most suited to whimsical fantasy designs where the soft, indistinct outline of animals or flowers, for example, on furniture, walls, or floors would fit into the feeling of the room itself.

STENCILING ON FABRICS

AND OTHER DECORATIVE OBJECTS

FABRICS AND STENCILING

In the Orient, skilled artisans were adept at creating elaborate robes stenciled in gold and embroidered with silk. Toward the end of the seventeenth century, the French stenciled and flocked ornate designs on fabrics that were hung as the first wallpapers.

Almost any fabrics can be stenciled. These can include fabrics woven from animal, vegetable, and synthetic fibers, but select them carefully and avoid textures that conflict with stencil patterns. Articles for home decoration, such as pillows, tablecloths, napkins, bedspreads, wall hangings, even draperies and curtains, can be made. Enthusiastic stencilers, with a minimum of expense, can produce original articles of clothing to include ties, blouses, or a floor-length party skirt. Stenciling dull clothes you seldom wear can transform them into the most appealing items in your wardrobe.

There is no limit to the designs suitable for fabric stenciling: florals, spots, borders, diapers, or bold geometrics used individually or in various combinations. Stencil designs can be copied and traced from wallpaper and other fabrics, or drawn yourself from any other source.

Color, also, can be as varied as you wish, but the color of the fabric will help determine the stenciling colors. One or more colors can be employed in the completion of the color scheme. The design can be stenciled in a lighter or darker shade of the fabric color, or in a contrasting one. Choice of colors and designs is really a matter of personal taste.

The following six steps should be read carefully. Both fabric yardage and ready-made articles can be stenciled using this procedure. Before attempting a major undertaking, I suggest a trial run-through on a small fabric remnant similar to what you will use. This extra precaution may save you from ruining a large amount of costly fabric. Stenciling on fabrics is a one-time procedure and errors cannot be corrected. If these six steps are followed accurately, the finished fabric will give maximum washability and durability, to say nothing of personal satisfaction.

PROCEDURE FOR FABRIC STENCILING

Step 1: Remove the Sizing

All manufactured fabrics are treated with sizing. Sizing is a glutinous substance used to stiffen the fabric by filling the pores of the weave, and it must be removed by washing the fabric with warm soap and water. Machine washing is fine for most fabrics but might not be for more delicate ones, which should be done by hand. If the material is ordinarily dry-cleaned, you must substitute that process for washing. Press the fabric while it is damp. When all wrinkles have been ironed out and the fabric is fully dried, begin step 2.

Step 2: Stretching Out and Marking the Fabric

Use a drawing board, work tabletop, or floor for your stenciling surface. Place several sheets of newspaper on the surface for protection. Place a sheet of white blotting paper on top of the newspaper. (Large white desk blotters can be purchased at well-stocked art or stationery supply stores.) The blotter will absorb excess color as the stencil medium penetrates through the fabric. Without a blotter, the colors will bleed past the outlines of the stencil plate.

Stretch a single thickness of fabric over the work surface and fasten with pushpins or thumbtacks. The fabric should not be stretched too tightly or pulled on the bias.

When the material is secure, use plain white chalk, colored dressmaker's chalk, or basting stitches to mark the location of stencil plates. Use a yardstick or measuring tape to determine the correct spacing. It is best to make as few chalk marks as possible when working with fabrics. Widely spaced dotted lines can replace solid lines and small x's or just a dot can mark the location of a spot stencil. Any remaining chalk lines that have not been painted over by stenciling will have to be washed or dry-cleaned out of the finished fabric. You may find that by gently rubbing the fabric together, the marks will disappear. If you use a loose, unknotted basting stitch with white thread instead of chalk to mark spacing, you can simply pull the thread from the fabric when the work is completed. Unfasten and shift the fabric as the stenciling progresses. Remember that a used blotter can bleed back into the fabric from underneath and must be changed regularly.

Step 3: Mixing the Colors

As described in "Making Your Own Stencil", page 29, there are two kinds of textile mediums. Textile silk-screen ink is a water-base medium, textile paint is an oil base. The range of available colors is limited—but you will find both primary (red, yellow, blue) and secondary (green, orange, violet) colors as well as black and white. By mixing your own colors you can create whatever tints or shades are desired. For example, red and yellow will give you orange, add white and you have coral; blue and white produce light blue, a touch of green will give you pale turquoise. For mixing colors, empty tuna-fish cans make perfect containers. Make sure you have enough of a mixed color to complete the article you are working on; it takes an expert to rematch a mixed color.

Silk-screen (textile) inks can be bought in half-pint cans and should be thinned to the consistency of light cream. Fewer silk-screen colors are available but intermixing the colors can produce any shade desired. Silk-screen textile inks are thinned with water and your brushes can be cleaned with soap and water.

Oil base textile paints come in jars and are sold as sets of various sizes as well as individually. Textile paints have their own thinner and cleaner but brushes may be cleaned in paint thinner; sold in jars, it must be stirred before using. The oil base textile paint must be mixed with an equal part of "extender." Extender is a chemical substance used to lighten the color and add permanency. Use as much extender as you need to lighten color since the addition of white to lighten the color further cuts down the washability of the finished work. Colors can be darkened by the addition of just a touch of black. Correct consistency is that of heavy cream.

Step 4: Stenciling the Fabric

Stippling is the best technique for fabric stenciling. Stippling brushes will vary in size. The largest is about one inch in diameter (no. 4) and the smallest ¼ inch in diameter (no. 1). Use a separate brush for each color. Work with clean hands, and as an extra measure to prevent any grease or dirt stains damaging the fabric, dust talcum powder over hands and stencil plate prior to starting.

Position the stencil plate over the chalk mark or basting stitch and tape in place. Hold it down firmly as you work. Dip your brush into the medium and pounce out on a newspaper palette. This will disperse the medium throughout the bristles and remove the excess. *The key to successful fabric stenciling is using a nearly dry brush.* A dry brush transfers the cleanest, sharpest impressions. Go over an area several times without recharging the brush. A single heavy application will clog the fabric and destroy the texture.

If more than one color is used, start with the color that will cover the largest area. Apply your second and third colors right after you have completely finished painting with the first color. If a stenciled area dries before the second color is applied for shading, the colors will not blend and you run the risk of stiffening the fabric with too much medium; therefore, the shading color should be stippled over the still wet stenciled design.

Step 5: Drying

Allow the finished work to dry thoroughly. The water-base inks take approximately fifteen minutes to dry. The oil base paint will not dry for several hours. When in doubt, overnight is a good drying period.

Step 6: Setting the Color

To make your stencil work colorfast, set your iron at medium heat (wool), place a dry cloth over the stenciled design, and press for three to five minutes. Turn the fabric over and repeat on the back. For fabrics such as rayon, nylon, etcetera, that must be ironed at a lower temperature, set the iron for warm heat (synthetics). Press this fabric for a longer period of time (ten minutes). Do not use steam. If the colors are not set properly, they will run when laundered or dry-cleaned.

A NOTE ON SPRAY STENCILING FABRICS

When using spray enamel, no color mixing is possible, but fabrics can be beautifully stenciled with the wide range of spray paint colors available. The object is to get the lightest coating of paint on top of the fabric. Avoid penetrating through the fibers. Spray enamel will stiffen any fabric through which it soaks. Remember to protect the surrounding areas. Spray residue cannot be removed from unprotected fabric. It is absolutely necessary, when spray stenciling on fabrics, to use spray adhesive on the back of the stencil plate or the paint particles will find their way under the ties.

For subtle effects of blending and grading color see both Spraying and Airbrush procedures on pages 37 and 48. Spray enamel is not the ideal spray medium for fabrics but it is permanent and colorfast when dry. Setting the color with an iron isn't absolutely necessary but will help to make the finished piece less stiff.

SOME HELPFUL SUGGESTIONS

White and light-colored fabrics tend to achieve more brilliant color effects. Stenciled colors are influenced by the color of the fabric you are working on. The textile medium at first will allow the fabric color to show through, and as the brush goes over an area several times, the color deepens until it is opaque. For example: red stenciled on a white fabric would show pink before it reached the red. Utilize these gradations for shading purposes and you will avoid mixing white with more intense colors to make pastels.

Note that black and other dark-colored fabrics will influence stencil colors. Red stenciled on a dark blue fabric (color plate 5) may look purple when finished (combination of red and blue is purple or violet). Pretesting color interaction between fabric and medium is necessary before going ahead. Note: Dark fabrics should be stenciled with silk-screen inks because the addition of white for lightening will not inhibit laundering or permanence of the finished piece as with textile paint.

On high-nap, or heavy-textured fabrics, such as mohair, velvet and thick wools, use strong patterns to complement the nature of the fabric. A thinner medium will make stenciling easier. Here do not try to penetrate the entire thickness of the fabric, because you might crush and mat the nap. To proceed, rub a lightly loaded brush gently in a circular direction over the nap. Take care not to pull the fabric out of shape with the motion of the brush. Hold the plate and fabric firmly with the left hand while stenciling. Keep the application light—if too much medium accumulates the fabric will be unpleasantly stiff and the paint might rub off.

Crocking, or the rubbing off of color, can be a problem and is due to excess medium on top of the fabric. Work the medium into the fibers of the material instead of just depositing color on top. You may have to work a little harder to achieve the depth of color desired but it lessens the possibility of crocking. Again, if you use a nearly dry brush and thin your medium if exposure to air has thickened it, you will avoid problems. If the stenciling medium hasn't penetrated the fabric, your design may disappear in the washing.

Some fading can be expected as time goes by. Clean your stenciled fabrics only when absolutely necessary. Like all colored fabrics, repeated washing wears down the resilience of the textile fibers. If you use a washing machine, set it for the gentle cycle and use a warm- or cold-water nondetergent soap. Handwash or dry-clean when required.

Standard and lightweight muslins are excellent fabrics for stenciling. Because they are more reasonably priced than most materials, large-size articles, such as bedspreads (color plates 7, 8) tablecloths, and wall hangings, are easily and inexpensively stenciled on muslin.

Embellishing a stenciled fabric can be interesting. The extra touch of a small basting stitch around the stenciled design will give added richness and appear to be appliqué at first glance. Use gold and silver thread for an elegant effect and perhaps a bright contrasting yarn if your pattern is a folk design.

This brings us to the possibility of using stencil designs as the base for needlework. The working surface—canvas or cloth—can be stenciled as for fabrics, giving instantly clear guidelines for crewel, embroidery, or needlepoint.

When some proficiency has been attained using the techniques described in this chapter, you can experiment with a more difficult form of fabric stenciling, which compares closely with batik, called "resist stenciling"; it is done on a white piece of fabric, and instead of using coloring matter as the stenciling medium, a removable, colorless substance like a cornstarch paste or melted paraffin is used. After stenciling is complete, the entire piece of fabric is submerged in a textile dye. The newly dyed fabric is allowed to dry and the resist is removed by washing, in the case of a paste substance, or for wax the fabric is ironed on top of a blotter until all the paraffin melts out of the fabric. In this manner the stencil design shows up white or the lightest shade, and the background of the fabric is the darkest color.

The supreme test for a job well done is not easy. Close your eyes. Pass your hand over the finished fabric. If you cannot detect by touch the part on which color was applied, you may congratulate yourself.

OTHER DECORATIVE OBJECTS

When Early American stenciling became fashionable in the latter part of the 1700s and early 1800s, every conceivable surface was stenciled. Museums and historical libraries throughout the New England states contain treasured examples of stenciled tinware, leather, clothing, glass, and paper.

Certainly fabrics, furniture, floors, and walls are most obvious for stenciling, but any material, if properly prepared, can become a stenciling surface. The following is a list of some of the possibilities.

Tinware and Metal

The name for painted tinware is tôle. In times past many household items made of tin were painted. At first, tinware was painted to protect it from rust, but then tôle work became a decorative art. Everything from simple metal canisters to elegant Chippendale tea trays was decorated in elaborate designs of fruits, flowers, birds, and shells.

Preparation for painted tin: Begin by washing the tin article with a detergent. Rinse with hot water and dry. Then apply a thin, even coat of val-oil and allow it to dry for twenty-four hours. Japan paint is best to use on tin. The desired background color should be mixed to the consistency of milk. Apply three coats of your background-color paint carefully, using an oxhair brush and allowing each coat to dry between applications. Sand lightly between coats. Protect the final coat with shellac. When the shellacked surface is dry, stenciling can begin.

Mark off placement with chalk, and tape the stencil plate in place. Japan or casein paints are good stenciling mediums. Any technique can be used. Tôleware was often painted black and stenciled with various shades of bronzing powders (see Bronze Powdering Procedure, page 46).

After the stencil work has dried, a good grade of varnish should be applied; at least three coats are needed to protect the decoration. Wet sand (see Painting Furniture, page 62) after the first two coats and lightly rub down the final coat with fine steel wool. The final step: Wax with a high-quality paste wax to achieve an eggshell patina.

Leather

Handbags, belts, wallets, or other articles made from leather can be stenciled. Stenciling on leather is often combined with tooling to emphasize the outline of a stencil design. Stenciled leather articles with fine-tooled designwork can be quite beautiful.

Suede, cowhide, pigskin, and kid are examples of various kinds of leather. Some are buttery-smooth while others are rough-textured. All leathers stencil well as long as the leather surface is not clogged with dirt or wax. There are many leathercraft stores that sell raw leathergoods and supplies.

If the leather you are working on is not raw or if there is any doubt, it must be conditioned. Leather conditioner is sold in shoe-repair stores along with shoe dyes. It is a chemical solvent that unclogs the pores of the leather so that color can penetrate and adhere properly. Saturate a clean cloth with the conditioner and wipe vigorously over the leather several times. When dry, the leather is ready for stenciling.

Use transparent stains or dyes in liquid form to keep your leather supple. The dyes supplied in shoe-coloring kits are fine for coloring leather. You can also use very fine oil colors from tubes, thinned with turpentine to a watery consistency for successful stenciling on leather. Stippling is the safest method of stenciling. With leather, make doubly sure that the brush used is nearly dry, otherwise the medium will seep under the stencil plate and ruin the leather.

Allow the finished work to dry for twenty-four hours. Tooling is done after stenciling. Spray on a final protective coating of silicone once all work is completed.

Reverse Painting on Glass

Until recent times, glass painting was fairly limited to church windows. But, as colonial people acquired more sophisticated tastes in home decorating and stenciling was fully accepted as a means of expressing color and design, plain glass came under the hand of imaginative stencilers. The clockmaking craft was developing in America about the same time as stenciling and the large round glass faces of banjo clocks were beautifully and creatively decorated. Today a mirror glass can be painted before being silvered, and the underside of a glass tabletop or, again, the inner face of a clock can be stenciled.

This unique form of glass painting is called reverse painting on glass. It has been practiced for hundreds of years. A design is applied to the undersurface of a piece of glass, in reverse form, that is visible through the outer surface in correct placement. Intricate, hand-painted designs in this technique are common, but simple stenciling will produce fascinating results. Clear Plexiglas or Lucite adapt to this process as well.

Clean the glass with soapy water and rinse. The dried surface is ready for stenciling. Some craftspeople prefer to coat the glass with clear gloss varnish to give a "tooth" to the surface, but I have found this distorts the clearness and yellows with age.

The mediums best suited for stenciling on glass are oil paint—thinned slightly with high gloss varnish and a touch of japan drier—or acrylic water paints. The consistency should be as thick as it comes from the can or tube, so it will adhere to the slick, nonabsorbent glass surface. Stippling and sponging are the most suitable techniques to use. They leave a pebbly semitransparent impression. It may be necessary to stencil a second coat if an opaque covering is desired. After the stencil work has dried several days, the decorated surface may be silvered, if a mirror glass, or fitted into place for use. No protective coating is needed.

Paper

The most common surface of all for stenciling is paper. It needs no special preparation —so long as it hasn't been waterproofed, it can be stenciled. Create your own stationery and greeting cards for birthdays and holidays. Quick and easy to design, stenciled paper is distinctive and pleasing to use. Party decorations take on a personal touch with stenciled placecards, favors, even napkins. Your own original painting on paper or fabric can be created with stencils. A painting composed of stencil design is called a theorem.

Use quick-drying water-base paint. On cards or a painting, spray the finished stenciled work with a commercial mat fixative, which is an invisible protection against fading and rubbing off.

And Why Not Cakes?

While researching for this book I discovered an old English stencil manual. It was written nearly a hundred years ago. The manual listed Royal Wedding Cakes as a stenciling surface. It described intricate, lacy stencil plates custom cut in designs especially meant for particular members of Royalty. Much like a doily, the stencil plate was placed on a frosted cake. Powdered sugar was then sifted all over the cake, and the plate was carefully removed, leaving a delicate stencil design. Here is the means to decorate a cake fit for a king and queen—or even you and me.

STENCILING ON FURNITURE

Furniture and Stencil Design

When one thinks of stenciled furniture, the famous nineteenth-century Hitchcock chairs probably come to mind. Many books have been written exclusively about them and, with their wide slats stenciled with gold melons, flowers, and leaves, these chairs are so popular that they are still being reproduced today. If you have an authentic piece of furniture of this period, you have indeed an original stencil design.

Furniture stenciling developed after floor and wall stenciling, and the first attempts were inspired by the highly fashionable gilded furniture abroad. French Empire furniture, designed at the request of Napoleon Bonaparte, was made from rich woods and had gilded mountings and brass inlays. In America, few could afford the luxury of imported furniture. Stencilers were quick to refine the art of stenciling with bronze powders in order to simulate the delicate patterns of French Empire inlays and mountings. Fancy chairs, pianos, and grandfather clocks made of rosewood and mahogany were skillfully stenciled with intricate designs that had the look of gold. These pieces were treasured and passed down through families, generation after generation. The Farmer's Museum in Cooperstown, New York, displays some of the finest of these pieces. Gradually stencil designs became less imitative of European styles and the distinctive Early American decoration evolved. Early American design reflected the simple, wholesome life of the times. Patriotic symbols of eagles and stars were a favorite, along with pinecones and weeping willows. The pineapple, symbol of hospitality, was popular and characteristic of a friendly people involved in the common struggle of building a new nation. Colors were sharp and clear with a strong preference for red, blue, and green. In this chapter, I do not attempt to cover historical reproduction that has been well documented by others, but to introduce the reader to stenciling as a most effective way to decorate all types of household furniture. Today's styles and tastes in interior decorating allow for a broader use of stenciling than ever before.

Painted furniture adapts particularly well to stencil design. Furniture finished in ivory or other light tints is very effective stenciled in contrasting colors. Dark backgrounds are well suited to stenciling in rich, vibrant colors. Gold design on black or polished wood imitates gilt and ormolu. Designs stenciled in black or ivory paint can suggest real ebony and ivory inlay.

All types of stencil design can be used to decorate a piece of furniture, and it is not necessary to reproduce a period feeling with stencils. Old and new can be combined imaginatively: a Louis XV chair or Victorian love seat upholstered in brilliant, contemporary print fabrics is very attractive. Likewise, period furniture can be stenciled in bold, modern design. Modern, straight-lined furniture can be combined with delicate arabesques, Oriental frets, or folk designs. Decorators and interior designers use this technique to add a dramatic touch to a decor. Today, the stenciler can make these combinations himself and turn out something with a totally new original effect.

Stenciling is possible only on furniture with a flat surface. A piece can be curved or beveled but should not have an overall covering of raised carvings or moldings. A period piece with sculptured cabriole legs and intricate carving may still have a top or panel suitable for stencil design. Tabletops, chests or cabinets, benches and chairs with broad slats, parsons tables and cubes, mantelpieces, inset panels on doors provide a wide choice of suitable surfaces. Artistic stenciling can transform an ordinary-looking piece of furniture into a work of art.

PREPARATION OF FURNITURE SURFACE

There are two common types of surfaces we will deal with in this chapter. The first is raw, unfinished wood furniture. The second is furniture with a finish already on it, whether it is paint, varnish, shellac, or wax. Each is prepared differently for stenciling, but the final results are the same.

Raw Wood

Whether the piece of furniture is a chair, table, or chest, it should be completely sanded with medium garnet paper until all edges are smooth and any whiskers of wood are removed. Dust the piece thoroughly with a tac-cloth to remove any sanding residue. Apply a thin, even coat of white shellac to partially seal the open pores of the wood grain. When dry (one hour), sand the surface lightly to remove the sheen. Sanding will also give a smooth surface for the first coat of paint or stain. Dust with the tac-cloth again and the piece is ready to be painted or stained.

Finished Wood

Use denatured alcohol to remove the wax on furniture that has been painted, or a wood finish that has been varnished, shellacked, or lacquered. If the clean surface— painted or stained—is in very good condition, you can stencil directly on it, or you can paint the surface in the background shade you wish after a light sanding and dusting.

When to Strip a Piece of Furniture

If the entire finish of a piece of old furniture is chipping, peeling, or cracking it must be stripped with a commercial paint and varnish remover before painting. Natural wood that has been finished with wax or oil rubbing must be stripped also. If you are in doubt about the type of finish, scrape gently over an unobtrusive part of the piece with a kitchen knife. If you are able to scrape off a white substance, it is shellac, varnish, or lacquer and need not be stripped. If no residue appears, it indicates an oil or wax finish that must be stripped.

Apply remover (stripper) generously with an old bristle brush. The finish will soften and craze. Protect your hands by wearing rubber gloves since the remover can give you a nasty burn. Remove the crazing finish with a paint scraper if the surface is flat. For carved or molded portions of furniture, use steel wool dipped in alcohol or lacquer thinner to clean out the turnings. Other helpful tools for getting all traces of finish and remover off the surface, especially if it has carved areas or ridges, are metal suede brushes, old toothbrushes, and, for deep carvings, orangewood sticks as used for manicuring. The application of remover may need to be done several times to strip the finish entirely. Be sure all stripping medium and finish have been removed, wiping the piece with fine steel wool and denatured alcohol, since any residue will prevent the new finish from adhering properly. Your stripped furniture can now be considered as a piece of raw wood and the directions for preparing raw wood should be followed.

STAINING FURNITURE

A raw or stripped piece of furniture is ready for staining only after a coat of shellac has been applied to seal the grain. The shellacked surface should be sanded lightly and dusted with a tac-cloth. A commercial *penetrating* oil stain is preferable to a pigment oil stain because the penetrating oil stain is a dye and penetrates deeper and more completely, leaving no pigment residue to clog the pores and grain of the wood. The stain is applied with a brush or rag. Rub it well into the wood. Remove excess stain with a clean, soft cloth. Take care to avoid streaking. Two successive coats should be enough to achieve the correct color depth. Let the stained wood dry thoroughly: twenty-four to forty-eight hours. After the stain is dry, brush on a thin coat of shellac and let it dry. The shellac layer is essential, since it will protect the background surface and prevent staining if you make a stenciling mistake that must be removed. You can now decorate.

PAINTING FURNITURE

After a piece of furniture has been shellacked, sanded, and dusted, it is ready for a first coat of paint. I strongly recommend the use of japan oil base paint. Japan paints are opaque, quick-drying and mat and can be used plain or to tint a good grade of flat white enamel for pastel shades. The correct brushing consistency should be that of medium cream; the paint is thinned with paint thinner. A good piece of furniture warrants no less than five coats of paint, with an absolute minimum of three. It is best applied with a fine oxhair brush, one to three inches wide, depending on the size of the piece of furniture.

Dip the brush into the medium halfway up the bristles, and press against the side of the container to draw off the excess paint. A too heavily loaded brush will cause drips and roll-overs. Paint is always applied in the direction of the grain. The strokes should be firm but light, to minimize brush marks. After a coat of paint has dried for twenty-four hours it should be sanded with fine sandpaper and tac-clothed. Add additional coats in the same way until the piece of furniture is completely enveloped in a "body of paint" that suggests depth. No wood grain should show through.

For a very smooth surface you must wet-sand. Sprinkle the painted surface with water, and sand with tufback sandpaper. Try to obtain satin smoothness. The surface is smooth enough if the raised brush marks cannot be felt. Wipe the surface clean.

When dry, apply a thin, even coat of white shellac. Allow the shellac to dry, and gently rub with fine steel wool. The painted surface is now ready for stenciling.

MEASURING AND TRANSPOSING DESIGN

After you have chosen your stencils, they may need to be scaled to the size of your furniture. When a design is either too small or too large in proportion to the piece, it will spoil the overall effect. Your own eye will tell you if the proportions are right. The design will appear to jump out at you if it is too large, and look ridiculously weak and shrinking if scaled too small.

Furniture surfaces and pattern sizes must be measured. Calculate the number of repeats and the spacing required. The design should be inset from the edge unless a diaper pattern is used. A curved or beveled surface should be measured with a cloth measuring tape and stencil plates cut from less stiff paper so they are able to bend with a curved piece and still lie flat.

A good starting-off point is to locate the center of the plain surface to be stenciled. Draw the horizontal and vertical center lines. This gives you the basis for drawing any additional guidelines. Since the corners of the stencil plates are cut at right angles, they can help serve as placement guides.

Draw chalk lines on the surface so they will bisect the stencil plate placed on top (*Fig. 18, page 22*). A latticework of chalk guidelines will give even greater accuracy when setting the plate. Stenciling is executed in an orderly manner. Start at the center of the design and work to the right and left, top and bottom, to assure evenness. Wipe off remaining chalk lines when stenciling is dry.

If the furniture is large, it can be moved about so that you can find the most comfortable and efficient working position. A chair can be laid on its back, side, or turned upside down for stenciling with greater ease. Tape can be used to hold plates in place, but since these furniture designs are usually small, a firm hand may be all that is needed.

SELECTION OF MEDIUM, COLOR, AND TECHNIQUE

The medium for furniture stenciling is a matter of choice. Any of those listed in the chapter, "Making Your Own Stencil," with the exception of textile mediums, will do nicely. I find the easiest to work with are either casein water paints or japan oil paints. (But first the piece of furniture has to be protected with a coat of shellac. A shellacked surface permits the stenciler to remove errors and start again without staining and discoloring the background surface.)

Mix casein paint with diluted white glue to a consistency of medium cream. Glue is added to ensure adherence of the paint to the shellacked surface. If you are using japan paint, thin it with paint thinner to the same medium cream consistency.

Acrylic paints are acceptable stenciling mediums but of less delicate texture. For decoration with metallic bronzing powders, the stenciling medium is japan quick size varnish.

Colors should blend with the decor of the room in which the piece of furniture will stand. But color combinations are as numerous as your imagination allows. Read the section on color in "Stenciling on Walls," which deals with the effect of Balance, Imbalance, and Neutrality; it applies to furniture as well as walls. A painted, stenciled piece can create a diversion and spark an otherwise staid decor. Colors of your painted furniture can add a bit of drama to the room, or they can blend in and bring the decor together.

Stippling, sponging, brushing, spraying, spattering, powdering can all be utilized for furniture stenciling either alone or in combination. Blending, shading, and highlighting procedures add depth and dimension.

Regardless of the technique chosen, the stenciling tool must be well pounced out on newspaper. It should be used as dry as possible because the medium is going to be thin. Try to render the design opaque while applying the least amount of medium to do so. When stenciling has dried for twenty-four hours, sand lightly with fine garnet paper to smooth any roughness in the application of the medium. On certain pieces where a semblance of age is desirable, sand the outer edges of the design so they appear slightly worn. The piece is now ready to be antiqued or protected with varnish.

A NOTE ON ANTIQUING A PAINTED PIECE OF FURNITURE

The purpose of antiquing is to create a patina that indicates long use and wear. The goal is to enhance a piece by suggesting age. When a piece is to be antiqued, the design must first be protected by a coat of shellac applied to the entire surface. The antiquing should be subtle. You can mix your antiquing by adding an earth color or black to some of the background paint. Add an equal amount to flat varnish and thin the mixture with paint thinner until the desired degree of transparency is obtained.

Brush a thin, even coat on only one side of the piece with an ordinary paintbrush. If you antique an area any larger, the antique medium will dry before you have time to remove excess for a subtler effect. The tool for removing antiquing is a 1½-inch-round sash brush, which can be purchased at an art supply store. Pounce the dry brush on the antiqued surface using the stippling stroke but more gently. Dry-brush pouncing will remove some of the antiquing medium. The procedure is done quickly with overlapping strokes so that a light, even antique is left on the furniture. Be sure to wipe the brush on a lintless rag after each stroke. A fast rhythm is worked out. When you proceed to other sides of the piece, constantly refer back to your first side to make sure you are matching the overall tone. No telltale seams or blotches should be apparent. When the antique has dried for twenty-four hours, you may proceed with the final varnish coats.

There are other antiquing techniques that should be considered. For these, consult books devoted exclusively to furniture finishing.

LEGENDS FOR COLOR PLATES APPEAR ON PAGE 8.

1

2

3

4

7

5

6

8

9

10

11

12

13

14

15

16

17

19

18

20

21

22

23

24

PROTECTING THE FINISHED PIECE OF FURNITURE

When all stencil work and antique is complete and dry, the finished piece must be protected. The most common protection is varnish. A high gloss, satin, or flat finish may be selected. In any case, use a high-quality commercial varnish diluted with 20 percent thinner. Do not dilute flat varnish, apply it directly from the can. Before proceeding, heat the varnish by placing the open can in a container of water that has been boiled. DO NOT HEAT WITH OPEN FLAME. Heating makes the varnish flow and minimizes unsightly brush marks. Apply the finish with a fine oxhair brush that is specifically used for varnishing. Your guide as to the number of coats of varnish applied will depend on how much wear and tear the furniture will receive in use. Somewhere between two and seven coats will be correct. Certain parts of certain pieces, such as the top of a bureau, can use several more coats of varnish for protection. Allow twenty-four hours drying time between coats. Remember that varnish is allergic to damp, humid weather. If possible, varnish in a dry dust-free atmosphere. Sand varnish lightly between each coat. After the last coat has dried, rub the surface with paste wax, to give it the polished sheen of a fine finish.

The following are four step-by-step treatments of stenciled furniture. The individual pieces of furniture are shown in the color plates and procedure is described here for each. Detailed instructions for every step are contained in this chapter.

ROUND DINING TABLE, GEOMETRIC WEAVE PATTERN

The round dining table (color plate 15) made of raw, natural sugar pine, was sanded smooth and dusted with a tac-cloth. A thin coat of shellac was brushed on to partially seal the pores. The table was stained with a penetrating oil stain of raw and burnt umber. A second protective coat of shellac was applied when the stain was dry. The stencil pattern shown in figure 33 was stippled on the shellacked surface. The curved border was

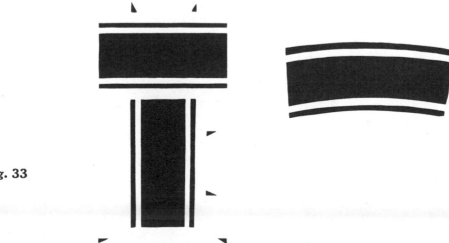

fig. 33

stenciled first. The first impression of the T-stencil was transferred at the exact center of the table but on one side of the center split. The small triangles served as guidemarks for the additional impressions of the T-stencil. When the T-stencil reached the curved border, a curved mask of cardboard was used to prevent the designs from running together and overlapping. The extra table leaves were stenciled last. The weave pattern of this stencil design is like a jigsaw puzzle; if the table was first stenciled with the leaves in place, upon their removal the design would no longer fit together. The T-design had to be stretched and placed farther apart on the leaves in order to make the weave appear unbroken. Ivory acrylic paint was the medium used. The stenciled table was varnished. Three high gloss coats were applied with sanding after the second coat and steel wool used to rub down the third coat and cut the shine. A final coat of wax was applied.

BLANKET CHEST IN FOLK DESIGN

While attending an auction I saw the old blanket chest (color plate 14). Someone had already gone to the trouble of removing the old finish and when I got the chest home, I began work at once. I washed the piece with denatured alcohol and applied a coat of shellac to seal the old wood. Only two coats of the base paint were necessary, and I sanded the surface very lightly so some of the brush strokes would show through the finish. After the base paint dried, the surface was shellacked. The spot and border stencil designs in figure 34 were combined and stenciled in different colors. When the stenciling was dry, all the stencil designs were heavily scuffed with rough sandpaper to expose the background paint and give the appearance of age. A brown antique was brushed on and pounced off with a dry sash brush. The dappled antique dried for twenty-four hours and two coats of flat varnish were applied. The chest was waxed after the last coat of varnish was dry. Friends who come to visit ask if the stenciled chest was passed down to me through the family. No one realizes the finish isn't as old as the chest.

LOUIS XVI CREDENZA, CONTEMPORARY STYLIZED DESIGN

I was hired to refinish the Louis XVI credenza (color plate 12). My client requested that the design be stylized from the upholstery fabric used in the same room. It was necessary to strip the old finish first. The stripped surface was given a coat of shellac as a binder for the succeeding coats of paint. Three coats of a pale grayed–green japan paint were carefully brushed on with light sanding between each coat. Then a thin coat of shellac was applied to protect the paint surface. The stencil design in figure 35 was

fig. 34

fig. 35

sponge stenciled in a darker shade of the same green on the top of the credenza. The stenciling on the drawers was modified from the top design to fit the space required. The fine crisscrossed lines were painted in blue–violet by hand. When the stenciling was dry, it was isolated by a coat of shellac. The entire piece was antiqued using the dark green paint and a touch of black mixed with flat varnish. The antique was brushed on lightly and pounced to an even speckled coating. A final coat of flat varnish was applied. When dry, the varnished surface was rubbed down with steel wool for smoothness and waxed to a satin finish.

LOUIS XV LADY'S WRITING DESK

The Louis XV lady's desk (color plate 23, 24) was found in an antique shop in New York, and although it is not an antique, the desk made an interesting project for stenciling. Several coats of poorly applied paint were stripped off, revealing—to my surprise—

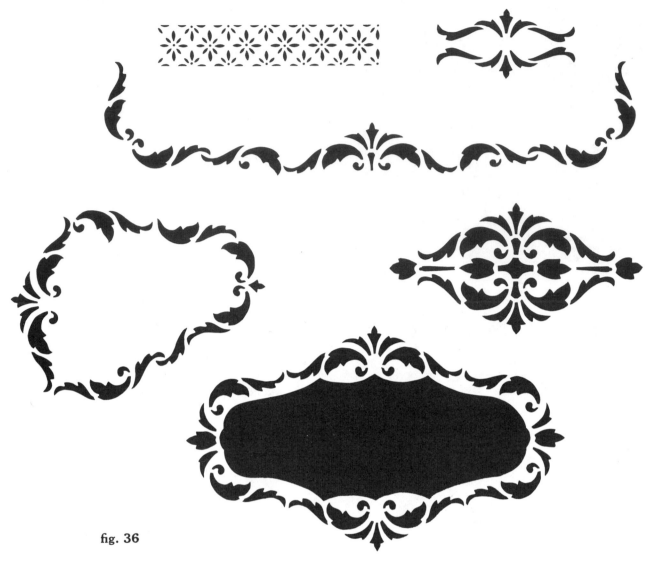

fig. 36

mahogany wood construction. A coat of shellac was applied to the stripped surface and five coats of flat black japan paint followed. Regular sanding was done after the second and fourth coats of paint, and wet sanding was done after the last. The smooth black surface was sealed with a carefully applied coat of shellac. The stencil designs shown in figure 36 were all modified from the medallion stencil to form cartouches that conformed to the lines of the desk. Talcum powder was lightly brushed over the area to be stenciled and the stencil plates were positioned. Japan quick size was then stippled on with a stencil brush and left to set for about ten minutes. With the stencil plate intact, a velvet bob dipped in gold bronzing powders was wiped across the surface. Several hours later a slightly moist cloth removed excess bronzing powder and talcum. The stenciled designs were shaded with warm brown oil paint mixed with varnish. The ivory stenciling in the center was stippled with japan paint. After the stenciling dried for forty-eight hours, varnishing was started. Three coats of high gloss varnish were applied with wet-sanding after the second coat. Each coat of varnish was allowed to dry for twenty-four hours and a finish coat of wax completed the desk.

STENCILING ON FLOORS

CREATING AN EFFECT WITH A STENCIL

Early American floors made of wide wooden planks were the first to be treated by stencilers. It is not known when the first stencils were brought to America, but it is probable that an immigrant painter, perhaps from England, introduced stencil decoration to the newly formed United States of America. In this country the "stencil era" began in 1775 and lasted through 1840. Homes then usually had a large central room, and in order to make it pleasant and interesting, stenciling became a popular form of decorating. Few people at that time could afford imported carpets or lavish decorating and, with the centralized room being used for cooking, eating, entertaining, and everything short of sleeping, carpets were impractical besides. Nonetheless, people of that era must have longed for the feeling that design and color could give to a room. Itinerant stencilers, traveling from town to town on horseback, provided a means of rapid and inexpensive decoration for floors and walls that appealed immensely to the Early American settlers. The first painted floors were spattered on a contrasting background in one color and finally several colors, creating a confetti effect. Spattering was superseded by geometric designs appearing first as borders and eventually as large overall patterns. Eventually, floor stenciling developed into great floral designs that covered entire rooms, creating the illusion of beautiful carpets. Floor coverings made of sturdy, waterproof sail canvas eliminated drafts and were extremely durable. These practical aspects must have appealed to the early New Englanders, who used canvas as floor coverings in their homes. Covered with colorful patterns of stencil design, decorated canvas floor cloths provided a way for a people of moderate means to have rugs and carpets. Stenciling was replaced when textiles and industry developed in America, placing woven floor coverings within the financial reach of everyone.

Today, every conceivable type of floor covering is available, ranging from natural and synthetic woven carpets to linoleum; tiles, stone, even grass can be simulated. With such an array of choices, it may not occur to us that stenciling a floor can often be the most exciting alternative. Stenciling a floor is the easiest and quickest procedure to master in this book and may result in the greatest sense of accomplishment. The simplest repeating stencil design or the most elaborate stencil pattern can change the look of a room dramatically.

PREPARATION OF A WOOD FLOOR FOR PAINTING

Preparation begins with scrubbing the floor and thoroughly removing all wax buildup. If this first step is neglected or done haphazardly, your paint will not adhere permanently.

Most commercial cleaners on the market are satisfactory. Wipe the washed floor with a rag soaked in denatured alcohol. The washed surface must be allowed to dry thoroughly and closed off from use. A wood floor takes twenty-four hours to dry or until the floor doesn't feel damp and cold. Any obvious cracks or holes must be free of dust and dirt and filled with plastic wood filler. A wood floor in very poor condition should be painted with a coat of paste wood filler and allowed to dry for twenty-four hours.

Any rough areas remaining on the floor surface must be sanded smooth. Small patches can be hand-sanded using a sanding block. The block can be purchased at a hardware store, or to make one, take a blackboard eraser or similar block of wood and stretch sandpaper around it. The sandpaper is turned up over the sides and gripped like a scrub brush. Sand in the direction of the grain. Of course, you must remove any powdery residue after sanding. Sanding is a wearisome process at best and I'm afraid the thought of having to sand an entire floor would discourage even the most dedicated stenciler. But if you must, rent a sanding machine for a day from a hardware store and enlist help. Fortunately, painting is an alternative to major sanding.

When the floor surface is ready for painting, the medium to use for background is heavy-duty enamel deck paint. White deck paint can be tinted with flat japan oil colors to a desired shade. Apply two coats with twenty-four hours' drying time between each. Use a wide house-painter's brush; stroke in one direction, usually with the grain of the wood. Deck paint has a thick consistency. Follow the manufacturer's instructions for applying. Take care to mask off floor moldings and walls with strips of masking tape or a piece of cardboard held in place as you paint near the walls. Of course, do not paint yourself into a corner. When the two coats are dry, stencil work can begin.

PREPARATION OF A WOOD FLOOR FOR STAINING

Sanding is the most important step in preparing to stain a floor. All old varnish, wax, or paint must be sanded off. A smooth, clean, and absorbent raw wood surface is required if a stain is to penetrate evenly. Using a sanding machine is the only practical way of accomplishing this. You will have to sand several times, with different grades of sandpaper. Start with coarse, then medium, then fine. A hand-held edger is the only means to get into corners. If you can afford it, have professional sanders do the job! Do not use wood fillers if possible, because the stain will be a different color in comparison with the actual wood.

A stain can be applied directly on the raw wood, but it is very difficult to get an even color. Use the commercially manufactured *penetrating tung-oil* stains. They come in a complete line of wood colors and can be mixed for custom color matching.

Stain is applied with a long-handled lambskin wax applicator soaked in the mixture. Wipe the stain across the floor following the direction of the grain. Wipe off excess with a dry soft cloth. For deeper color, leave a stain longer before wiping. Try to stain quickly, avoiding any overlapping as you proceed as it will deepen color unevenly. Again, floor moldings and walls should be masked. When the stained floor has dried for twenty-four hours, the process can be repeated to darken. A stained wood floor will absorb paint into the grain and leave a shadow when the paint is wiped off. Although it should not be necessary, you may shellac a floor so that stencil mistakes can be removed completely.

PREPARATION OF LINOLEUM, MARBLE, AND TILE FLOORS

These surfaces differ from wood in that they are nonabsorbent. If you paint directly on them, the paint will chip off. Therefore, after the surface has been washed to remove any wax and dirt, apply a coat of val-oil. Val-oil is a strong varnish commonly used for priming metal before painting. A coat of val-oil gives the nonabsorbent linoleum, tile, or marble a bonding surface. It is stroked in one direction with a large brush. Let dry for twenty-four hours. Your surface is now ready for two coats of enamel deck paint to be applied twenty-four hours apart. When the floor is dry, stenciling can begin.

PREPARATION OF A CANVAS FLOOR CLOTH

Weight no. 8 canvas can be bought by the yard in various widths. Only your largest art supply stores will stock a canvas as heavy as this. Even a canvas manufacturer who supplies canvas backdrops for theatrical productions may not stock no. 8 weight, but he may have remnants. Try to find a width that will not require cutting the finished edge or sewing pieces together. Finish off cut edges by turning a hem under no more than 2 inches and gluing it together. A cut edge may be purposely unraveled to form fringe. Protect your floor with newspaper and lay the canvas on top. Anchor temporarily with steel pushpins or tacks along the edges. Then apply three thin coats of enamel deck paint twenty-four hours apart in the same manner as has been previously described. Begin your stencil work when the canvas is dry.

COLOR AND DESIGN

A floor is firm and strong. Colors and designs you choose should be in keeping with the character of such a surface. Shading, highlighting, or blending, which have the effect of three-dimensional projections and hollows, are unsuitable for floor stenciling. A flat design executed in solid colors will suit a floor best. The pattern or motif can be an abstract or realistic, geometric or floral, or combination of these patterns, but your designs should have strong general form.

Select a background floor color in harmony with, but darker than, the walls and woodwork. Colors chosen for stenciling and striping should harmonize with the background color and not contrast too strongly. Usually, two stenciling colors and the background color are enough. If more are desired, tints and shades of the two stenciling colors can be utilized. Color creates an effect. Vivid hues or pale pastels can be chosen in accordance with the decor. The darker and more closely related the colors, the more subdued and subtle an effect it will have. If colors are light, bright, and contrasting, the effect will be intense and vivid. Avoid stenciling with a color at its full intensity on a very pale, weak background because the design will jump out at you and you will be tired of the effect in no time.

Consider the mellow, aged tones of old Oriental carpets, the almost faded, pale pastels of the Aubusson rugs, and the neutral earth shades of beige, sand, ivory, and brown that are so beautifully combined in the Moroccan floor coverings. Navajo Indian rugs have touches of black, white, reds, blues, and yellows on a neutral beige or gray background. A little historical research will spark the imagination and provide you with ideas for your own color and design schemes.

MEASURING AND TRANSPOSING ON A FLOOR

Regardless of the design you have chosen—border, diaper, or spot—prepare a graph of the floor to scale. Measure the length and width of the floor including any alcoves. Reproduce the shape of your floor in scale. Mark windows and doors in their correct location.

The scale drawing should indicate important features of the decoration in correct position, such as: the location of a border, the positions of repeated spot stencils, or the exact placement of an all-over diaper pattern. Experimenting on graph paper will also help you determine the relative size of different stencils combined in the same scheme, such as: a border combined with spots, a border interrupted by principal parts, spots of various sizes, or diapers combined with borders. A certain amount of variation in size is desirable, but should never look discordant. Use your eye to determine what is acceptable balance. If you work out problems of scale beforehand, you will have no unexpected surprises or disappointments later on (*Figs. 38 and 39*).

When the scale drawing is complete, use it to show where to place chalk guidelines on the actual floor.

The most accurate way to transfer a long chalk line to the floor surface is to stretch twine or string taut between two tacks where the line will be. Tape can be used instead of tacks, but allow for the width of the tape when you determine the placement of the line. A straight line is formed that can be traced on the floor with chalk. Remove the string and continue to the next setting. Repeat this procedure until the entire floor is crisscrossed with chalk lines. In this manner, all lines can be transferred to the floor without confusion.

Stripes, which are painted on a floor to enclose a border stencil or terminate a diaper before it reaches the wall, will vary in width but are rarely less than 1 inch wide. To make a 1-inch-wide stripe, draw parallel chalk lines on the floor 1 inch apart. Attach long strips of masking tape to the outer edges of the parallel chalk lines, isolating the 1-inch-wide stripe. Paint between the two strips of tape. When the paint is dry, remove the tape and you are left with a perfect 1-inch stripe.

Try to utilize the narrow wood slats of equal width on hardwood floors as straightedges to follow, and also as guides in determining the intervals between a repeating design. A parquet floor is even better since the surface is already graphed for you, permitting easy location of any design.

BORDER STENCILING

Border stenciling is a band of continuous design used to accentuate the shape of a room. It is the easiest pattern to stencil. Border stencils are also effective as an outline for an area rug. You can either create the effect of a rug or just a border around the edge of a real carpet. Borders for floors should be simple, strong, conventional designs—geometrics of straight or curved lines. The size of a room will determine the width of a border. You may have to do a little scheming to select just the right width. Working this out on a scaled graph will simplify the procedure. Borders should be placed at least 8 inches from the wall; a foot or more in larger rooms. Borders can have a width of 2 to 3 inches, 4 to 6 inches, 8 to 10 inches, even as much as 18 inches.

Begin by transferring the first impression at the middle or center of a chalk line that marks the location of the border. Opposite parallel borders will always match symmetrically if you work out from the middle of each. Place the next setting to the right, continuing until the last setting of the stencil brings you to within a foot or so of the turn. Then, go back to the center and repeat the procedure to the left. Stencil all four sides in like manner, leaving the corners to be finished last.

At the corner the stencil should look as if it continues around the turn. With further regard to corners, there are a number of choices available to the stenciler. A turn-corner is a separate stencil that has been adapted and slightly modified from the border design. It is a design to make a right-angle turn and flow uninterrupted into the border design. A second alternative is to use a spot stencil at the corners. The spot design can harmonize with the border, but it is not necessarily of the same motif. It should, however, be larger in width than the border so that it overlaps. The third and easiest solution is to continue the next setting and miter the corner. To do this, mask the stencil plate at a 45-degree angle at the point where the intersecting borders, coming from different directions, join. When stenciled, the border will abut against the opposing border, forming an oblique angle, but will not overlap. Mitering can be easily understood by observing how a picture frame is joined at corners. The drawback to this method is that the lines of stencil design do not always meet. But the intricacy of pattern and the neatness of a mitered corner can make the finished appearance acceptable (*Figs. 12, 13, 14* in the chapter on Stencil Design).

Borders are often set between two solid stripes. When the space enclosed by a border is to be spot- or diaper-stenciled, you may wish to define the border by striping. The color of a border and the area it encloses may be different shades of the same color, producing the effect of a rug (*Fig. 37*).

SPOT STENCILING

The treatment of floors with spot stencils is somewhat akin to diaper stenciling. A scale drawing must be prepared and the floor carefully laid out with a diaper of transverse chalk lines as guides. The spot stencils are transferred over the intersections at regular intervals. Various-size and -shape spots can be alternated. Spot stencils vary in design: pure geometric, floral, or combinations of both. Be careful that the stencil is in keeping with the character of a floor. The floor anchors a room, supporting all that is above. When stenciling is complete, wipe off remaining chalk lines. You should have a pleasing disbursement of regularly spaced stencil designs (*Fig. 38*).

If spot stenciling is applied wall-to-wall, your effect will be that of an inlaid floor (color plate 10). If you stencil wall-to-wall on a painted floor surface, the floor will have a carpeted look. Stencil designs applied inside a border will give the appearance of an actual area rug. This is particularly true if the background color contrasts with the color of the space that separates the border from the wall. A stenciled area rug is pleasing in all variety of shapes: oblong, square, diamond, oval, round, or free-form.

The more adventurous stenciler may want to try the interesting, delightful look of *trompe-l'œil:* the art of fooling the eye at first glance. As an example, on a large expanse

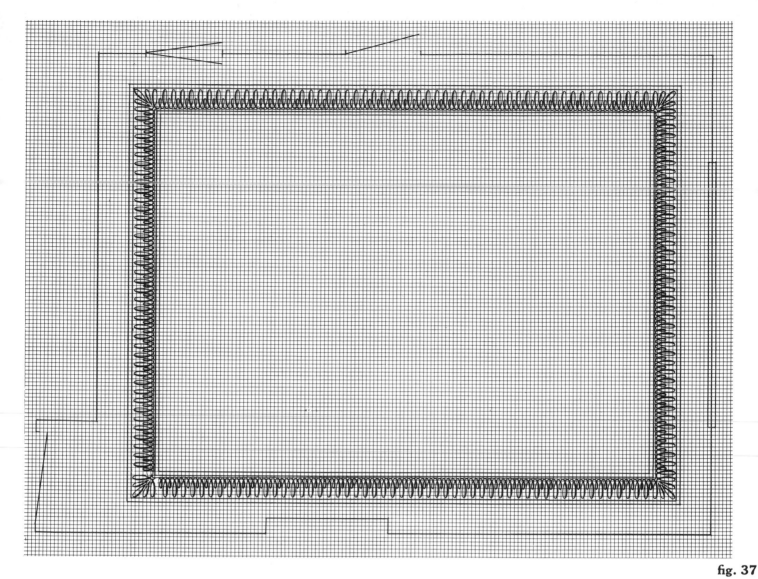

fig. 37

fig. 38

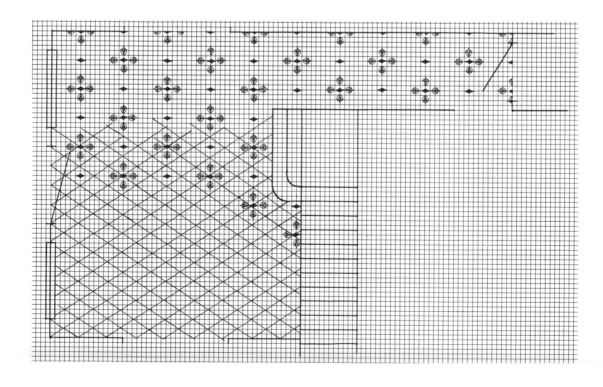

of stained wood floor surface, stencil scatter rugs in unusual patterns and finish them off with stenciled tassels. Stencil scatter rugs of different shapes and sizes in the same room, but do not use too many. You can imagine the delight when surprised friends realize, at second glance, that your rugs are the hand-painted work of an imaginative stenciler.

DIAPER STENCILING

Diaper stenciling is a much more complex form of stencil design. The components of the design continuously repeat themselves, forming an overall pattern. The effect is one of a beautifully patterned carpet. Diaper stenciling can be used to imitate the French Savonnerie and Aubusson rugs, and Oriental carpets with their intricate tapestry designs.

A diaper is a repeated design. It can consist of simple lines or a complex, interlocking pattern. The stencil plate should contain at least one complete setting of the pattern. Stencil the first impression, then stencil additional impressions to the right, left, top, and bottom. Continue until the floor is entirely covered with design having no apparent beginning or end (*Fig. 39*).

Diaper stenciling can be a combination of border and spot stenciling. Regularly spaced chalk lines are laid out on a floor in a simple diamond or square diaper pattern. The transverse chalk lines are stenciled with narrow bands of design or painted as solid stripes and become part of an overall pattern. Next, spot stencils are centered inside the diamonds or squares and stenciled repeatedly until the entire floor is covered with design.

Sometimes diapers are even more complex. They can be based on interlocking hexagons, octagons, and circles, as well as diamonds and squares. Combinations of borders, spots, and diapering are endless. A diaper can be enclosed by a wide border. An oval border can be set inside an oblong border and the two separated by a diaper design (*Fig. 40*). Likewise, circles can be set inside squares, squares inside circles, diamonds inside ovals, etcetera, with diapers separating the two borders. This technique is used to reproduce the appearance of the French and Oriental carpets mentioned above.

A floor can be stenciled in a pattern resembling handsome ceramic tiles of delft and in larger more colorful Persian tiles (color plate 9) as well. Do a little research. Many books and magazines on interior decorating have photographs of beautiful rugs and carpets. Study them and adapt the shapes and patterns to your own taste.

Do not begin to diaper a floor unless you have prepared a scale drawing. This is described in more detail on pages 72–73. By experimenting on graph paper, you will be able to: (1) determine correct proportions in relation to the room, (2) decide on what combination of borders, spots, and diapers you would prefer, (3) select the proper designs, and (4) resolve spatial density of the diaper itself. This preparation for diaper stenciling may be complex but once you begin to stencil, it is smooth sailing.

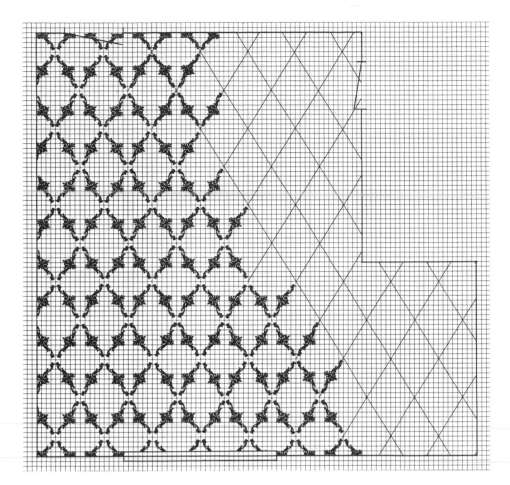

fig. 39

fig. 40

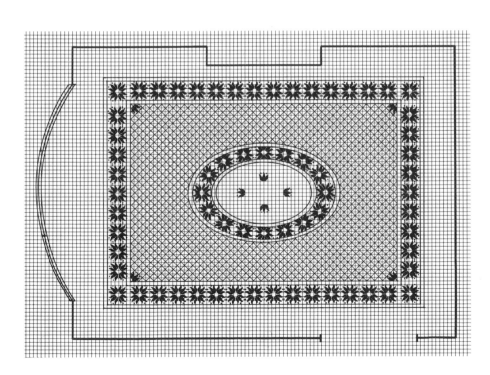

FLOOR CLOTH STENCILING

Stenciling a canvas floor covering is exactly like stenciling a floor. Any of the techniques I have already mentioned can be utilized. A no. 8 weight canvas floor cloth can cover an entire floor, wall-to-wall, or be cut to the size of an area rug. American Indian or Primitive African designs adapt exceptionally well to the rough texture of heavy canvas. For the same reason, a delicate floral or fragile lacy design would not be fitting on this coarsely woven fabric. Floor cloths are best suited for dining rooms, living rooms, or hall runners (color plates 17, 18).

Acrylic or oil base paints should be used. When a floor cloth has been protected with varnish, it can be cleaned and will wear better than most carpets.

SELECTION OF MEDIUM AND TECHNIQUE

Choice of medium is optional. I recommend either japan oil base paint or water-base acrylic paint because both dry quickly and have a flat finish. Casein paint is also suitable. The paint should be thick. A thinner consistency will also work but greater care must be taken in its application.

Before you start, clean the plate and your hands, then lightly dust them with talcum powder. Wear clean working clothes and lint-free socks with no shoes. Stencil plates should be made of sturdy paper board for maximum durability. Tape the plate in place and begin stenciling. Pick the plate up carefully to check your work and then transfer it to the next given place. If you make an error in spacing or painting, quickly and carefully remove the wet paint by wiping with a rag dipped in the paint solvent.

Because the most appropriate stenciling on floors consists of simple, strong design, the technique must correspond. Texture is not desirable. Solid, opaque color is the most suitable choice. The stippling technique achieves complete coverage quickly and a #10 or #12 brush is best. Try to get an opaque covering with the thinnest coat of paint possible because any raised ridges of paint from textural applications (sponging, brushing, etcetera) will wear unevenly. Stipple with a lightly loaded brush. Pounce out the brush on newspaper until uniform paint coverage is apparent. Paint should start to appear mat before you are finished stenciling.

Another technique for floor stenciling is spraying. Commercial spray enamels are tough and durable. Be sure to mask off surrounding areas with newspapers. Spray enamels take a few minutes longer to dry than other mediums but are quicker to apply.

If more than one color is used, stencil the entire floor in the first color before starting the second color. Use a separate brush for each color. Concentration and effort in measuring and application will result in a beautifully stenciled floor.

PROTECTING A STENCILED FLOOR

All painted stencil work must dry for twenty-four hours or the final application of varnish will dissolve and smear the design.

The procedure for protecting painted or stained floors is the same. Heavy-duty polyurethane floor varnish is applied, 2 parts satin and 1 part high gloss, with a minimum of two coats required. On a dry day, apply the varnish in a warm room that is as dust-free as possible. Allow twenty-four hours drying time between each coat. Waxing with a good paste wax is the last step. A floor cloth requires four coats of varnish but is not waxed. Maintain regular floor care. Some wear can be expected in time that will erase the newness and enhance the look of the floor.

STENCILING ON WALLS

As described, in the early American home first thought was given to stenciling floors, but wall stenciling developed rapidly and extensively. With stenciling considered most fashionable, it was not unusual to see stencil design applied throughout an entire home. Some of the original stenciled walls that are preserved today tell us that two effects were sought after. One was the elegant French drawing room with border stencils of swags, tassels, and ribbons and panels of delicate flowers and leaf sprays. Oftentimes this style of stenciling was an obvious attempt to copy formal wallpaper designs. The second effect was simplicity itself, combining gay and romantic designs in clear, realistic colors. Bright red berries and hearts, crisp green leaves and vines, multicolored flower baskets with soft blue and pale yellow flowers spill over walls in a way that is uniquely charming. Both effects are different but each reflects the distinct taste of early America. Progress and the industrial revolution, with its assembly-line manufacturing, brought on the decline of stencil decorating. Mass-produced domestic wallpapers replaced stenciling. Today, stenciling has returned with a much wider range of application. Interior decorators have made astonishing use of the boldness and graphic simplicity that stencil designs possess. Stenciling is often reserved for those who hire an artist, and more often than not a decorator is involved. But because stenciling is surely one of the easiest of the artistic crafts, any amateur can effect professional results almost immediately, and almost any kind of room can be enhanced by some sort of stenciling. It is a matter of individual taste, whether one wishes to reproduce the Early American stenciled wall or to stylize any object in a room and continue the feeling on a wall.

WHAT MAKES A WALL?

A wall can consist of any number of sections (*Fig. 41*). Starting from the ground up they are:

Floor Molding or Baseboard. The strip of wood meeting the floor at the base of the wall. The molding generally retains the background color or perhaps is painted solidly in one of the stencil colors. It is never stenciled.

Dado. A section at the lower broad part of an interior wall just above the floor molding. The height can be anywhere from twenty-four inches off the ground to just over halfway up the wall. The dado is usually stenciled in a design that is vertically dominant and repeated, so that it will give visual support and strength as a base for the filling, frieze, and ceiling.

Dado Band or Rail Border. This stencil design is just above the dado and is contained inside two horizontal lines. The dado band is used to accentuate the place where the dado ends and the filling starts.

Finial Border. A finial is an ornamental termination. Combined with the dado band, the finial border is usually a stencil spot jutting up from the band at regular intervals.

Filling. The largest area, comprising most of the wall. The filling is stenciled in spot or diaper stencils or large verticals widely spaced. Located between the dado border and the frieze, the filling can contain repeating patterns or central motifs. When there is no dado treatment, vertical stripes of design at least 18 inches apart will give the desired feeling of support.

Drop Design. A reverse finial border, the drop design is combined with the frieze design at regular intervals, dropping down from it.

Frieze. A border that terminates the filling and performs the same job as the dado band and dado. The frieze is stenciled in a continuous horizontal theme but is narrower than the dado.

Cornice. The molding at the top of the wall meeting the ceiling can be of actual wood (three-dimensional) and is treated the same as the floor molding. If there is no molding, the cornice can be stenciled in a design different from what was used for the frieze and narrower.

Of the above, with the exception of the filling, all are continuous designs repeating themselves. You may use all of them or any combination.

Structural and architectural work must conform to the rules of good construction. Therefore, in choosing the stencils for your walls, the base design should always appear stronger than the design placed on top. Lighter color and less rigid design can be used as you proceed farther from the base.

The following treatments are for those persons who are fortunate in having a home with uncommon architectural features:

Lunettes. The area framed by an arch or vault should be treated with special care. Stencil with one main large spot and smaller related designs surrounding. The design should always conform to the shape of the space.

Spandrels. The area framing an arch can be stenciled with a border surrounding the arch or in a cornice and rail border, underlining the curve of the arch.

Pilasters and Columns. There are a number of ways to handle a shallow rectangular projection from a wall. If you do not wish to accentuate the projection, stencil in the same manner as the rest of the wall, continuing the borders, bands, dado, filling, etcetera, as if the projection weren't there. If you do want to accentuate the form, reverse the color scheme, reverse the design, change the design, or center something on it (*Fig 42*).

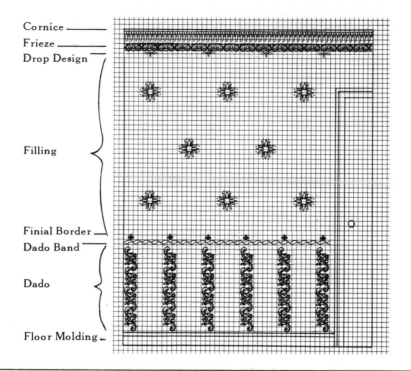

Cornice
Frieze
Drop Design

Filling

Finial Border
Dado Band

Dado

Floor Molding

fig. 41

fig. 42

THE INDIVIDUAL ROOM

Whether you decide to stencil only one wall or all the walls in a room, you must first have an idea of the atmosphere you want to create. Any kind of distraction on a wall, whether it be stenciling, wallpaper, pictures, or draperies, will tend to make a room appear smaller. The object is to bring the room together but not down on top of you.

Certain rooms and the way they are decorated suggest certain themes. You must evaluate the size of the room, the furnishings, the fabric patterns in your upholstered pieces, the draperies, and the carpet. You can formalize or informalize a room by your choice of stencil. You can reproduce an Early American kitchen or a Victorian boudoir. A primitive Indian motif can accent a few treasured pieces you possess. A child's room can come alive with the stuffed animals that adorn the bed. Stenciling in a bathroom can pick up towel or shower-curtain designs, while you can avoid the tiresome patterns in commercial bathroom wallpaper. A particular architectural feature, such as a mantlepiece or fireplace, can be elaborated through the use of stencils.

Simplicity and geometrics seem to be the key to modern stencil designs; florals and curves to quaintness. If you have a room filled with lovely antiques and heirlooms you would not want a bold geometric pattern, but a floral pattern would be charming. Likewise, if your decor includes chrome and Plexiglas predominately, a bold geometric design might be just right to enhance the simple but beautiful contemporary lines of the furniture. A room that is overlarge and sparsely furnished can be made to appear smaller and cozier by choosing an intricate design and increasing the density of stenciling on all four walls. A dark, depressing room is made cheery and light by an occasional interesting spot stencil combined with the right colors. Rooms with particular purposes, such as kitchens, breakfast nooks, and porches are charming and pleasant when stenciled with beautiful borders of tulips or morning glories to greet you.

The following helpful suggestions can guide you when dealing with certain types of rooms that you wish to stencil. They are designed to modify or accentuate certain architectural features.

In small rooms with low ceilings, the walls and ceiling should be tinted the same light shade. Stencil designs should be of a delicate but simple, open pattern. If possible they should all run vertically with no horizontal bands interrupting. This will give the ceiling the appearance of being higher. If an overall vertical is not to your liking, a narrow cornice border, pale in color, and similar band located just above the baseboard and door casings is an equally attractive treatment. Any three-dimensional molding at the ceiling level is painted the background color of the wall so as not to define the limits of a low ceiling (*Fig. 43*).

The opposite is true of small rooms with high ceilings. The ceiling and the top area of the walls can be tinted a slightly darker shade than the walls, causing the ceiling to appear lower. Use horizontal bands at different levels on the wall to break up the large expanse of wall space. The stencil design can be bold and well defined (*Fig. 44*).

Stenciling in large rooms with high or low ceilings offers an opportunity for a greater variety of wall treatments. Somewhat darker background colors can be utilized. Vertical and horizontal stencil design can be used together. All-over diaper patterns can cover a wall or be broken up with a contrasting dado or frieze. Latticework stencils are well adapted to large, spacious rooms. Walls can be subdivided into panels (*Fig. 45*).

No matter what size or shape the room, the applications are endless. The choice is yours.

fig. 43

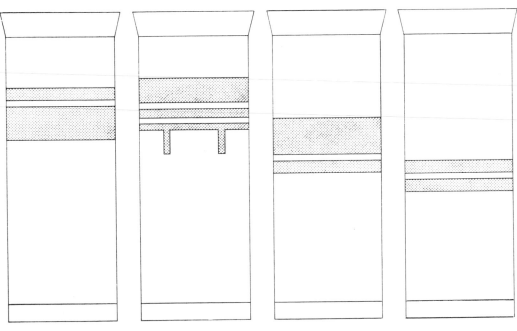

fig. 44

fig. 45

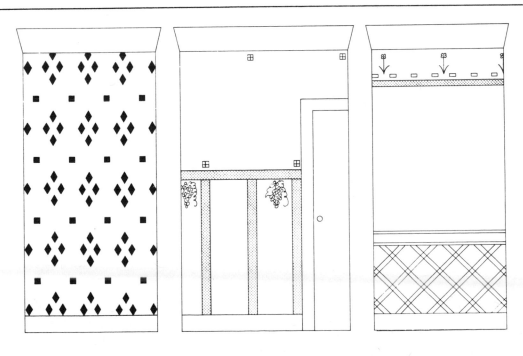

A NOTE ON CEILINGS

When a theme is continued onto a ceiling the design should be strong, firm, and geometric, regardless of the form the design takes on the walls. Ceilings are designed to support an upper floor in addition to covering an apartment or room. Possibly the lines can form an interwoven texture, leaving an impression of strength with lightness—strength for supporting an upper floor, lightness for the cover over a room. Design on a ceiling should not outweigh the design on the walls supporting it.

Stenciling should be attempted only when you are absolutely set on it, as it is very tedious and time-consuming work.

A simple alternative for stenciled ceilings is a straight-line, inset border. Decide how wide the stripe should be and how far away from the wall you want it. An example would be a 3-inch-wide stripe set 12 inches away from the wall. Take a piece of cardboard and cut a rectangle 12 inches by 15 inches (12 plus 3 inches). The cardboard rectangle is called a template. Climb a ladder with a piece of chalk and the template. Place the template flat against the ceiling with the 15-inch side adjacent to the wall. With the chalk, mark a dotted line against the outer edge of the template, parallel to the wall. This will give you a line 12 inches away from the wall. Turn the template around so that the 12-inch side is adjacent to the wall and mark off with chalk the outer edge, which will give you a line 15 inches away from the wall and running parallel 3 inches out from the previous chalked line. Follow this procedure around the room. After you have finished, take a roll of 1-inch masking tape and attach long strips to the outer edges of the two parallel chalk lines to isolate the 3-inch border. Press the tape as flat and secure against the ceiling as possible or paint will get underneath. When you have gone around the whole room with the tape lines, you can start to paint. Use a brush or natural sponge dipped in paint for a more textured effect. When the paint is surface dry, carefully peel off the tape and you are left with a beautiful inset border (*Fig. 46*).

PICKING COLORS WITH CARE

After the design is chosen, color is the most important factor. Early craftsmen used primary colors mainly—red, blue and yellow—with no perspective or shading. The colors you pick will influence greatly how your pattern turns out. Colors interact on each other and your choice can make a stenciled design recede into the background or stand out from it. (Color can affect people psychologically—shocking, soothing, even depressing.)

Colors fall into four main groupings: warm, cool, neutrals, and earth. Warm colors are reds, yellows, oranges and their derivatives. Cool colors are the blues, greens, and some-

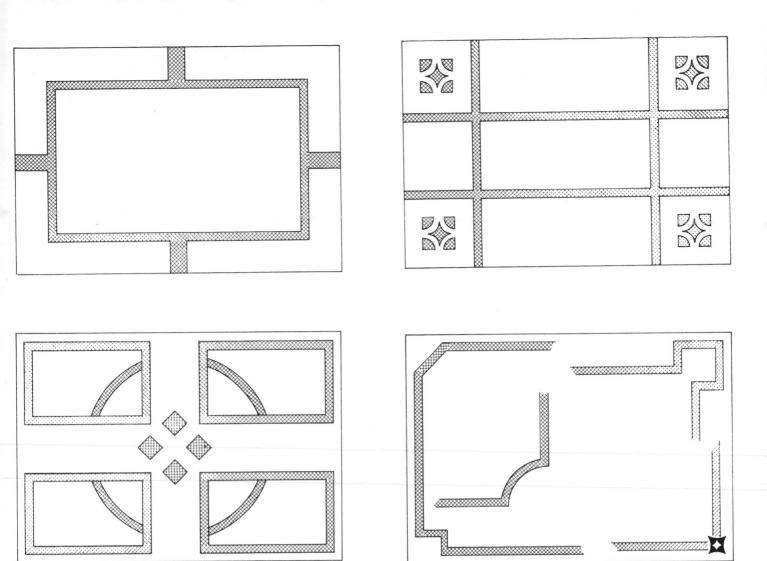

fig. 46

times purple. Neutral tints are devoid of color—white, grays, and black. Earth colors take in all the browns.

For backgrounds, I prefer light grounds but not a pure white. I think stenciling gets lost on a dark wall or at best looks unusual. The choice of colors you stencil with may be chosen easily from the objects in the room: fabrics, furniture, art, carpets.

There are certain classic color approaches to a room. The most common is two main colors: e.g., on walls with the majority of a stenciled design in a smoky taupe color, apple-green, stenciled sparingly throughout the taupe design, could provide accent. Perhaps you would have a light gray background stenciled in a medium yellow, with accents of bright Chinese red or ivory.

A monochromatic color scheme includes *varying* tints and shades of the background color; a pale pinkish background color, and stenciled designs in tints ranging from pinks through rose to deep burgundy. When using a monochromatic approach, wipe-out stenciling can be most effective, adding depth and perspective to the design.

Another classic treatment is white with one color. I tint the white slightly with whatever color I am using for stenciling to cut the sharpness of pure white. The off-white becomes the background and a soft wedgwood blue can be used as the stenciling color. A long vertical design, combined with a cornice border and deleting the dado, brings out the lovely simplicity of this combination.

Real objects such as flowers and animals can be stenciled in realistic colors as in nature, or fantasy colors where your imagination takes over. When you stencil a design with a color at its full intensity on a weaker background, the design will jump out at you. That may be the intended effect. But it is a good thing to remember that color varies greatly in different light. What you stencil that looked perfectly lovely on a cloudy afternoon may reveal a circus attraction next sunny day.

Pick your colors according to the effect you wish to create in a room. The effect of BALANCE is achieved through the use of warm and cool colors together, or light shades with darker shades of the same color. If the room has good dimensions with no architectural faults and no furnishings that particularly dominate the scale, balance is the ideal way to stress good points. Use a monochromatic scheme or pick two colors from the fabrics in the room, one warm and one cool. Example: For a room with a deep green carpet and upholstered pieces and draperies in golds, greens with rust and turquoise trim accents, choose pale green background on walls (cool color) and stenciled design in rust (warm color). In this situation the color scheme imparts a feeling of ambience.

A different effect is obtained through IMBALANCE. Overstress the intensity of a color or two or emphasize the density of stencils covering a wall. In a room with awkward dimensions and glaring architectural faults, this technique is best suited. To make a long room seem wider, lighten the two side walls and ceiling, and darken both end walls with a shade of the same color. To heighten a room, paint the ceiling the same shade as the walls instead of white. A room with a row of small, unattractive windows or too many doors will benefit by overstressing color and design, bringing the eye away from the disturbing elements. Utilize this method to overcome the monotony of a room.

NEUTRALITY is created with the use of closely related colors or neutral tones. Choose this effect when you want to make a wall inconspicuous, blending in pleasingly so as not to detract from the actual furnishings of the room. A room with numerous paintings, collections, or treasured pieces of furniture should not be overshadowed by the wall decoration.

PREPARATION OF THE WALL SURFACE

Painted Walls

Preparing a wall surface for painting is simple. Preparation amounts to washing and painting a wall. I prefer flat paint surfaces, except in the kitchen and bathroom, where necessity may demand a glossy surface to expedite repeated cleaning. In these rooms, high or semigloss enamel wall paint is preferred. Any commercial latex or flat enamel wall paint is fine on all other walls.

Wall paint, glossy or flat, can be easily applied with a roller or brush. I prefer to use a roller, but if you wish to use a brush, take care to paint in one direction, up and down, to avoid leaving unsightly brush marks.

A wall doesn't necessarily need to be freshly painted before stenciling. If you are satisfied with the present color, just be sure the wall is completely free of any dust or grease. Vacuum it, or use any commercial cleaner when you wash your wall. Needless to say, peeling or flaking paint, cracks, and holes should be repaired before any attempt at stenciling can begin.

Prepare your room in its entirety before starting to stencil. Paint the walls in the background color you have chosen and allow to dry overnight. You can stencil over wallpapers in good condition after the surface has been painted.

One technique for painted walls that those with a little more daring and experience than the beginner might want to try is blending. It gives the background some added texture and depth. I suggest you practice first on a sample board before attempting a wall. Do not work on more than 4 square feet at any one time until you gain speed and dexterity.

In blending, two similar or harmonious colors, such as a very pale yellow and a slightly darker shade of yellow, are applied on a light-colored or white wall surface and mottled together as follows:

Dip a coarse natural sponge into the darker color and pounce randomly on the wall. Slightly more than 50 percent of the space you are working on should be covered in this manner. Dip a second natural sponge into the lighter shade and pounce it over the remaining unpainted surface, partially covering the first color. No unpainted surface should be left. Immediately, a third sponge wrung out in the solvent of the paint used is pounced over both colors until they start to blend pleasantly. A dappled mixture of both colors with highlights of the individual colors should be apparent. Pouncing is executed lightly and quickly. As you continue along the wall, make sure you are achieving the same effect everywhere and there are no obvious checkerboards to tell of your progress. Blending gives a delightful, soft, muted tone to a room, and is best combined with a minimum of stenciled design, perhaps just an inset border at cornice and baseboard and around door casings. Ultimately, three shades of a color can be used, even harmonious colors such as pinks and blues mottling to mauve, or green and ivory. A blended surface dries overnight.

Wood Walls

Preparing the surface of a wood wall is simple also. Wash the wood down with denatured alcohol or lacquer thinner to remove any wax or grease. Transparent mediums, such as stains, are the most effective because they allow the natural grain of the wood to show through. Somehow, opaque paints in contrast with the bare wood lack a feeling of consistency. The commercial 4-by-6-foot and 4-by-8-foot wood panels are sealed with lacquers and have little evidence of graining, making them nonabsorbent and unsuited for stenciling.

MEASURING THE WALL AND LAYING OUT THE DESIGN

The first step in visualizing and testing out your stenciling ideas is to lay out rooms to scale on a piece of paper. This way you can easily work out the problems beforehand, taking into account the location of doors, windows, the size of the stencil, number of repeats and connections. Do this on graph paper if possible. If you are stenciling more than one wall in a room, line them up adjacent to one another. The drawing will give you a general idea where to begin. The chief pattern and its smaller borders or bands must be in proportion to each other and to the wall space. Wall lengths and pattern sizes are measured. Calculate what spacing each requires, how many repeats, what happens at corners, at doors, and window frames. It is interesting to note that early craftsmen did not regard spacing as important and often ended with leftover space they just arbitrarily filled with anything.

The next step is transferring chalk guidelines onto the wall. Mark off the horizontal and vertical center lines of each wall regardless of where your designs will go. The transfer is accomplished by coating a sturdy string with chalk and holding it taut against the wall. An assistant is extremely helpful. The center of the string is then pulled a few inches away from the wall and snapped against the wall, leaving a straight chalk line. Use the string both vertically and horizontally. If you are working alone, the chalked string can be held between two outstretched arms, a loop tied in the center, pulled out with the mouth and released.

On vertical measurements a plumb line will determine the true vertical. Walls rarely measure accurately, showing the importance of having chalk lines carefully laid out by measure, which can be followed with the stencil plate. While vertical center guidelines must be determined by measuring, any horizontal molding (with the exception of floor molding) can be used as a substitute horizontal guideline. Place chalk lines where any horizontal bands or borders will be stenciled (dado, dado band, frieze, cornice, etcetera).

In the case of vertical bands, measure the wall distance on either side of the center vertical guideline. Divide that distance into equal parts, taking into account the width of your stencil designs and the distance you want between them. Example: An 11-foot wall with a center vertical at 5½ feet (or 66 inches), a stencil design width of 6 inches. Try

6 verticals on either side of the center, divide 6 into 66 inches and the centers of the stencils will be spaced 11 inches apart. Taking into consideration your stencil would be centered over the vertical, it would overlap each side by 3 inches (half the width of 6 inches) leaving a dividing space of only 5 inches between. This would be unbalanced. So we drop down to 4 verticals; 66 inches divided by 4 is 16½ inches apart. The overlap of 3 inches on either side of the vertical leaves a space of 10½ inches between stenciled patterns, a nice balance. Never stencil a vertical pattern in a corner, the corner defines itself. Begin transfering your vertical chalk lines 16½ inches to the right and left of the center vertical and continue. A scaled graph here is extremely helpful.

When stenciling an all-over spot or diaper design on a wall, run chalk lines both vertically and horizontally, crisscrossing each other at regular intervals. Use the method described above to determine the correct measurements. Lines can also be diagonal, starting with a big X as your center guide. The X can go from corner to corner although it is not prerequisite. In an all-over diaper design these true chalk lines are especially important. A line that is off as little as ¼ inch at one end will be way off at the other, causing a mismatch. Once these guidelines are drawn accurately, diaper and spot stenciling proceeds very quickly. Center the stencils over the intersecting chalk lines. Mark the stencil plate with center lines up and down so that when placing the plate on the wall they line up with or run parallel to the chalk lines.

Certain stencils—bands or borders for example—are very easy to work with without regard to spacing, except the last link or two may have to be shortened or stretched to meet the first one. The continuous, repeated design in these stencils can be likened to the links of a chain. Often they are used for the dado band, cornice, and simple frieze. I find it easier to work from the right side of the wall to the left. These stencils are the first I do on a wall, being the easiest and fastest to complete.

Other, more complicated stencils consist of continuous design bands broken regularly by a larger motif. Finial borders, friezes with drop designs, and frieze and cornice borders that have a different design interrupting the flow of the band pattern are called interrupted borders. Consider carefully the spacing of these stencils. The principal parts of the design should appear at regular intervals along the wall. A principal part should never end in a corner. The band portion of the stencil connecting the principal parts may have to be stenciled more often than the larger motif to achieve good balance and spacing. In going around the room with this type stencil, I center the principal part over the center vertical line and transfer the first impression. Place the next setting to the left continuing until the last setting of the stencil brings the principal part within a foot or so of the corner. Then, go back to the center and repeat this procedure to the right. Stencil all four walls in this manner, leaving the corners to be finished last. At this point the stencil plate can be creased to carry the continuous band around the corner.

If you are stenciling fewer than four walls you must visually terminate your bands, borders, dado, frieze, etcetera. Borders do not just end unless they are very narrow. The simplest method is a vertical stripe. A pattern can be modified, but in any case it should appear definitely terminated.

Attach and secure the stencil plate to the wall while you stencil. Pins were commonly used but I think they leave holes that cannot be easily hidden. I use a special type of masking tape called drafting tape that is not quite so sticky. Drafting tape is applied to the edges of a stencil plate and taped right to the wall. Take care to line the stencil up with the chalk lines. Tape should not be placed over freshly stenciled surfaces for fear of peeling paint off. After stenciling, the plate is carefully and slowly removed to avoid smearing the paint or ripping the stencil.

SELECTION OF MEDIUM AND TECHNIQUE

Having decided on your colors, designs, and the atmosphere you want to create, choose your medium carefully; it also can affect the look of a room. Almost any paint, ink, or stain can be used for wall stenciling. The most practical are water-base paints because they dry quickly and you can proceed rapidly. Stencil plates can be placed immediately overlapping the previously stenciled area in a continuous design. I suggest casein paint for a flat finish and acrylic paint for a slightly semigloss finish resembling oil paint. Both mediums are opaque. Japan oil paints are excellent and can be mixed with flat white enamel to any color desired. Japan paint dries to a flat, opaque finish also; a glossy finish can be achieved with it by the addition of undiluted high gloss varnish. All the mediums listed should be mixed to a fairly thick consistency, as heavy cream. Stains and inks have their drawback in the fact that they are a watery consistency and are harder to manage. Watery mediums are tricky on a vertical wall where a too heavily loaded brush or sponge will drip behind a stencil plate and down the entire wall. Stains, of course, are the most transparent of all mediums and have a beautiful effect. On a semi- or high gloss enamel wall, use acrylics or japan paint because any other medium would be repelled by the nonabsorbent surface and would not bond well.

Technique is optional on walls too. Stenciling with stippling brushes that solidly fill in the design area can be used when the design itself needs little embellishment. When a sparse or simple design covers a wall, sponging can be pleasant because it adds texture (color plate 19). Highlighting, shading, and wipe-out stenciling enhance many stenciled patterns. You can experiment on plasterboard or Masonite before working on the wall directly.

Spray painting is fast and effective, but take special care because on a vertical wall one spray too much or too close will cause a drip. Enamel spray paint does not dry quickly enough to transfer your stencil plate one right after the other. Newspaper should be used to protect the top, bottom, and side areas from the spray residue.

APPLICATION

Keep the paint fairly thick. If you have mixed different colors to obtain a particular shade, strain the finished paint to assure complete mixing. I use a piece of nylon stocking stretched over a container and a spoon to push the paint through the mesh. Lumps of the individual colors are thus forced to mix and you will avoid the uneven transfer of color to the wall.

Pounce out your brush on a newspaper palette to disperse the paint through the bristles. Use a separate brush or sponge for each color, making sure they are clean and dry at the start. Do not try to replace a stencil plate over a wet impression to correct errors. Wait until dry to do so. Lay down your brush while you remove the plate. Loosen the tape first at the sides and then at the top, finally pulling it straight away. Avoid sliding the plate against the wet paint and smearing your finished work. Continue stenciling around the room to completion.

Complete all continuous designs before stenciling spots. In multicolor work, the predominate color is stenciled first and completely finished before second and third colors are started. When a stencil plate showns signs of buckling or moisture absorption, allow the plate to dry or use a new one. Overloading your brush or using too thin a medium will cause the plate to deteriorate more rapidly. Be sure you are stenciling crisp, clean impressions. When edges become blurry and indistinct, it is time for a new stencil. No protective finish is needed over the completed wall.

SUPER-
GRAPHICS

I became interested in supergraphics when I was decorating my New York apartment. Interior decorators were designing custom supergraphics for their clients, and after seeing the lively effect a supergraphic created, I decided to design one (color plate 4) for my living room. My supergraphic took three days to complete and added just the right finishing touch to the room.

My definition of a supergraphic is a line drawing of gigantic proportions that almost borders on pop art. No shading is involved although simple perspective can be utilized to create the illusion of depth and dimension. Colors are rendered flat, solid, and opaque. Perspective was used in figures 47 and 48. In the first figure, the silhouette of the face was redefined twice. By using the darkest color in the face and progressively lighter shades in the second and third outlines, the face will appear to advance toward you. The second figure makes a small room appear larger. Distant mountains, a receding highway, and falling shadows make you feel as though you could travel up that road. Painting this supergraphic with pale, realistic colors will cause the changing light in the room to simulate dawn, hot midday, growing darkness, and finally moonlight. In both these instances, the illusion of depth and dimension is achieved without using the artist's traditional methods of shading and highlighting.

A supergraphic can cover part or all of a wall and extend onto the floor or ceiling. The supergraphic has many uses—enlivening a humdrum room decor, influencing the size of a room, or just an inexpensive alternative to wallpaper, mirrors, etcetera. Perhaps the most artful use of all is camouflage. An ugly wall with too many doors, a wall radiator, exposed steam or water pipes, all can be disguised by making them disappear into the supergraphic.

In a friend's apartment, where the entrance opened into the kitchen and all guests had to march through it to reach the living room, a supergraphic drew attention away from the usual kitchen fixtures. The kitchen was painted off-white and three bright, harmonious colors were combined to form a striped band 12 inches wide that encircled the room. From a bull's-eye in the center of the floor the band went up one wall, across another, over doors, around a window, and over kitchen cabinets until it reached the living room where it burst into a giant tricolor arrowhead. Guests were so entranced by the flowing design and bright colors, they followed the arrow right into the living room without a glance at the kitchen.

PLANNING A SUPERGRAPHIC

When the particular room and wall have been chosen, the next step is to decide on the subject of the supergraphic. Subject matter for a supergraphic can be taken from anything. The design can be stylized, realistic, or fantasy; a pure geometric design, floral, animal, or scenic. The only rules regarding supergraphics are that the design be of gigantic proportions and no form of shading or highlighting be utilized. To shade or highlight can turn a supergraphic into a wall mural or fresco and, unless you are an extremely good artist, the results will be amateurish. The solid, opaque and distinct colors in a supergraphic are vital and refreshing.

Oftentimes doodling on a pad of paper will give you the first idea you need. Then you must enlarge the theme and balance the results. The supergraphic in the color plate and corresponding figure (49) started with a doodled star and one arrow. Additional arrows, a pinwheel, and a free-form cloud behind the star were added to enlarge the theme and balance the design.

Balance is the most important part of a supergraphic. A person looking at a finished design should not feel his eyes being drawn to any particular area. The largest parts of the design may be grouped in one area making the supergraphic appear top-heavy or one-sided. Balancing a supergraphic is similar to making a floor plan and arranging the furniture. You do not line all your furniture against one wall leaving another wall bare; instead you disperse the furniture throughout the room in a balanced manner.

Take the length and height measurements of the wall surface. On a sheet of graph paper, use a convenient scale, such as 8 squares to a foot, and plot the measurements. Indicate where doors, windows, cabinets, and furniture are located. Using the same scale, make cut-outs or templates of each part of the design. Use solid-colored paper for the cut-outs so they stand out from the graph paper. Move the cut-outs around until you arrive at an arrangement that appears balanced and doesn't draw the eye. By doing this bit of paperwork, it will become apparent whether certain parts of the design should be scaled down or enlarged. Trace the final location of the cut-outs onto the scale drawing (*Figs. 47, 48 and 49*).

Choice of a color scheme is a matter of personal taste. Begin with the colors already established in the room, such as upholstery fabrics, carpeting, draperies, and furniture. The colors in your supergraphic should harmonize with the surroundings.

Color also has an effect in balancing the design. Studying the color plate, the pinwheel on the right side was painted a darker more intense color (cranberry) to balance the busier left side of the supergraphic design. The dark orange and turquoise in the star were the accent colors in the room along with deep yellow. To avoid introducing too many colors, I used tints of the same colors: coral, pale turquoise, and light yellow. Since the majority of the design colors were warm, I chose a cool background of pale blue to achieve a balance between warm and cool colors.

After you have finished the scale drawing of your supergraphic, place a piece of tracing paper on top and experiment with crayons or pastels until you reach a pleasing disbursement of colors. Read over the section on color in "Stenciling on Walls".

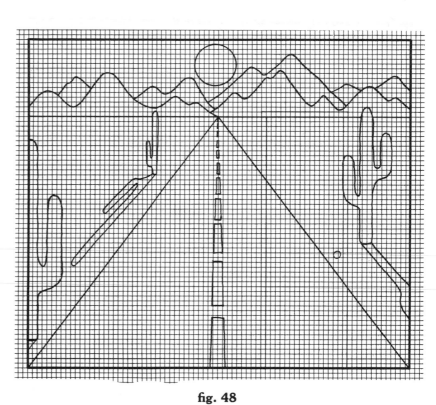

fig. 47

fig. 48

fig. 49

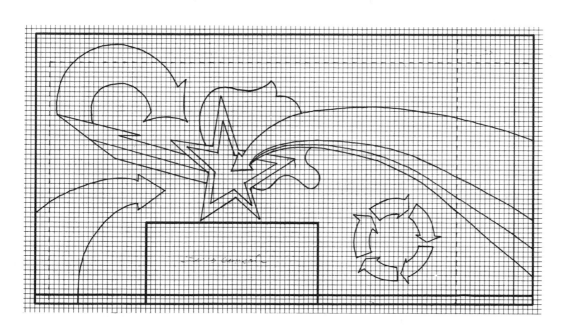

MEASURING THE SURFACE AND TRANSPOSING

The wall, floor, or ceiling surface must be washed clean of all dirt, grease, or wax. Fill all cracks and holes and sand smooth. A fresh coat of paint is not necessary. Since the supergraphic shown in the color plate had such a great deal of blue background color surrounding the design, it was easier to paint the entire wall first and then paint the design over the blue. Some touching-up may be needed with this method to cover any pencil marks still showing.

Use the scale drawing of your supergraphic to tell you where the designs are drawn on the wall. The exact location of the design components is determined by translating the number of squares per foot on your graph into feet and inches on your wall. Mark the location of any furniture to be placed against the wall.

Use a sharp pencil to draw the design on the wall surface. A light, wooden yardstick, aluminum pushpins, string, and an art-gum eraser are all the tools you will need.

Most compasses are not large enough for the gigantic proportions in a supergraphic design. A simple alternative is a piece of string, looped at one end, and anchored by a pushpin. The opposite end of the string is tied to the pencil. The length of string between pushpin and pencil becomes the radius of a circle. Hold the pencil perpendicularly to the wall and pull the string taut. As the pencil travels from point to point an arc or circle is drawn. Free-form curves, such as the pale yellow area behind the star in color plate and corresponding figure 49, are drawn freehand. Use the eraser to remove the incorrect pencil marks after sketching freehand.

Straight lines are drawn using the wooden yardstick. Lines longer than 3 feet can be drawn by stretching a piece of string taut between two pushpins and then using the string line as a guide for the pencil.

To avoid cracking plaster, take special care when it is necessary to hammer an aluminum pushpin into the wall. Nails can be used also, but upon removal, the resulting hole must be filled and sanded. Use a sturdy stepladder to reach upper wall areas.

TAPING

Taping is an art. The crisp, clean lines of some abstract art were achieved with careful application and removal of plain masking tape. A book could be written just on the effects of masking tape on twentieth-century art. Painting a supergraphic would become arduous and time-consuming if taping hadn't been developed.

Masking tape comes in varying widths and is easily bought in any houseware or hardware store. I use ¾-inch or 1-inch tape. Masking tape has just the slightest amount of stretch with excellent adhesion. Use a stencil knife or razor blade to trim excess tape when necessary.

Masking tape must be in secure contact with the surface that is to be painted. Apply the strips of tape close to the pencil marks but not over them. Run your fingernail along the tape edge that will come in contact with the paint to make sure no ripples remain. One long, continuous strip of tape, unrolled as you proceed and pressed in place, is better than several short strips. Paint can seep under the tape where the strips overlap. Nothing is more disconcerting than removing the tape and finding a messy, illegible line that has to be touched up or done over entirely. Tape will have to overlap at intersections and angles, so extra care is taken securing the tape to the surface at these points.

Taping a curve is more difficult than taping a straight line. To tape the inside of a curve, the edge of the masking tape that will come in contact with the paint is stretched slightly to follow the curve. The inside edge of the tape will form ripples. The ripples of excess tape are pressed together and against the surface leaving no air pockets (*Fig. 50*).

Taping the outside of a curve is harder. The masking tape must again be stretched to follow the pencil line. But this time the limited stretchability of the tape makes it necessary to rip the opposite edge at regular intervals in order to follow the curve smoothly. With the tape pressed securely against the surface, no pockets of air are evident (*Fig. 51*).

The object of taping is to isolate a particular component of design in order to paint it. Tape all the design areas to be rendered in a single color before going on to the next color.

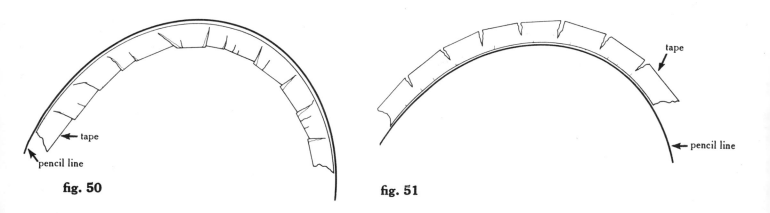

fig. 50   fig. 51

PAINTING

The most easily used medium for supergraphics is the commercial latex wall paint. Latex is fast-drying, water-base for easy cleaning, and covers solidly with one coat. Latex is so widely used now for interior house painting that manufacturers have developed a palette of vivid colors as well as pastels and white. Half-pint, pint, and quart cans of latex paint can be bought in any paint store and colors can be custom-matched if you do not care to mix them yourself. Supergraphics that continue onto a floor surface should have that portion painted with enamel deck paints.

For most work I use an ordinary 1-inch-wide paintbrush. Smaller and larger width brushes can be utilized also. Brushes are cleaned with soap and water.

The masking tape is placed a slight distance from the pencil line. When the taped-in area is painted, the medium will cover the pencil marks. Now use the paint line to guide the placement of the tape for the adjacent color. Indent the tape slightly so the second color overlaps the first color. Painting should proceed from the lightest color to the darkest, thus avoiding the need for a second coat of light paint to cover a darker paint. Tape can be stripped off immediately following painting. Several hours drying time should be allowed before taping over a newly painted surface.

No protective coating is needed on a wall surface. Latex wall paint is washable when dry. A supergraphic extending onto a floor surface is prepared and protected using the methods described in the chapter on Stenciling on Floors.

A SELECTION OF STENCIL PATTERNS

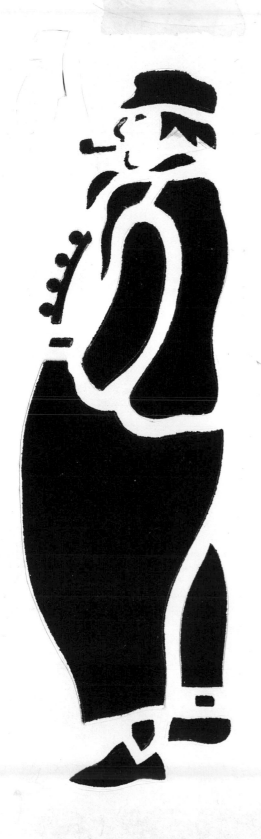

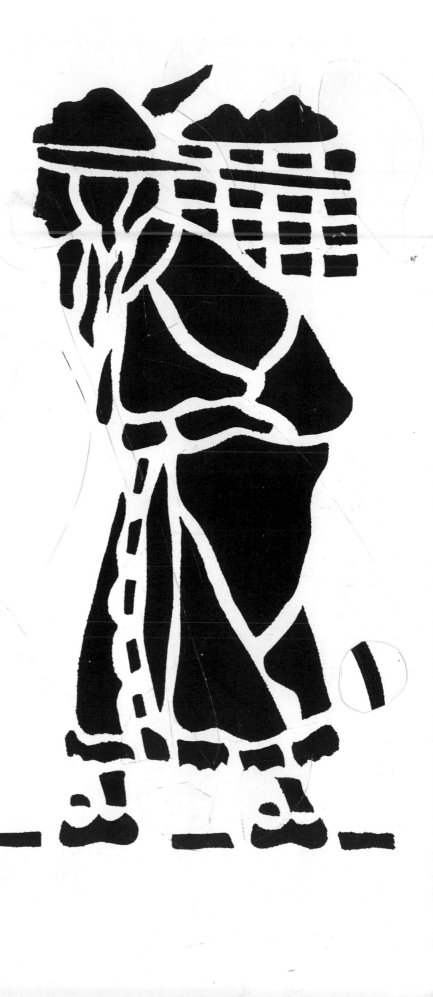

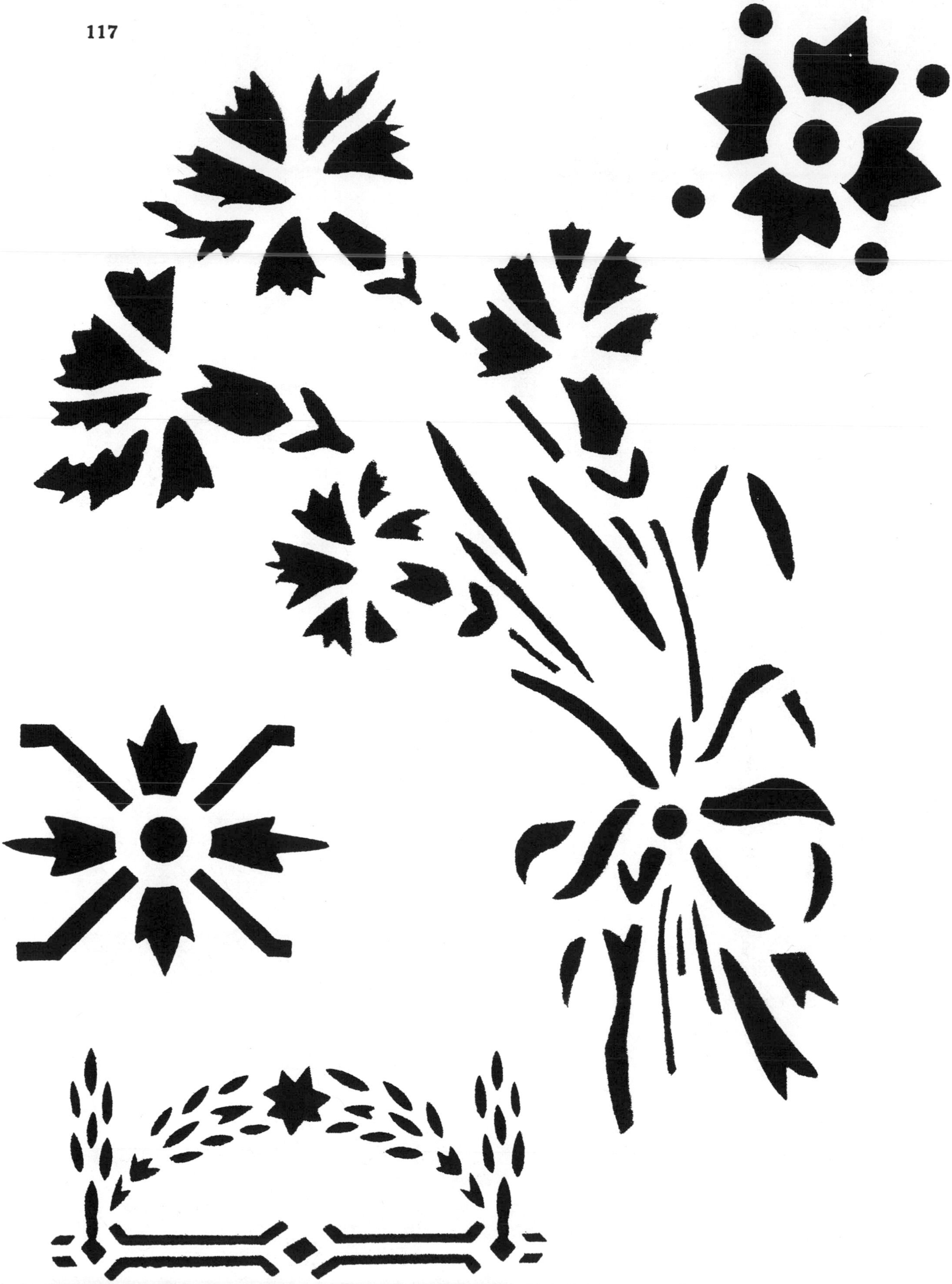

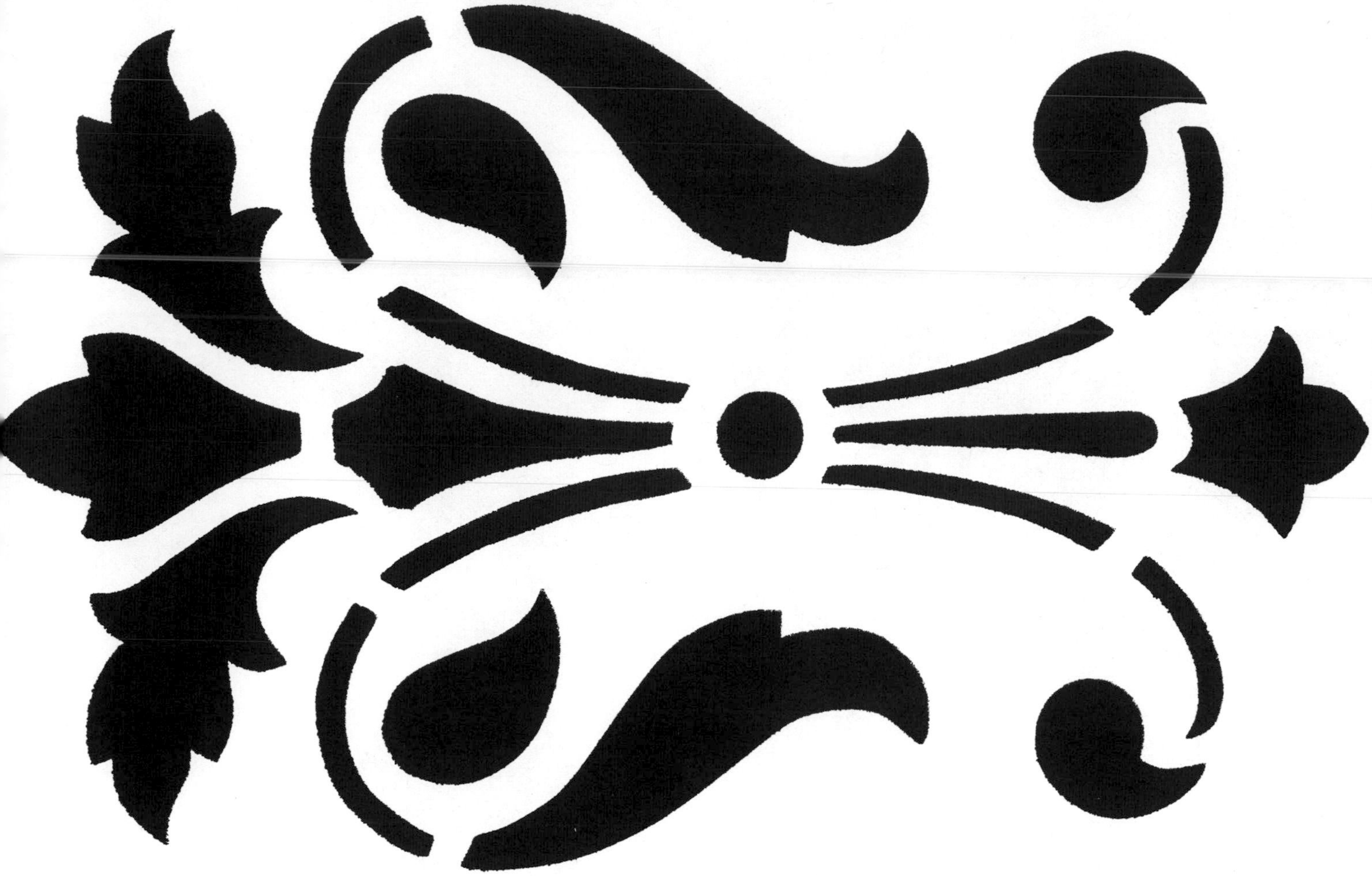

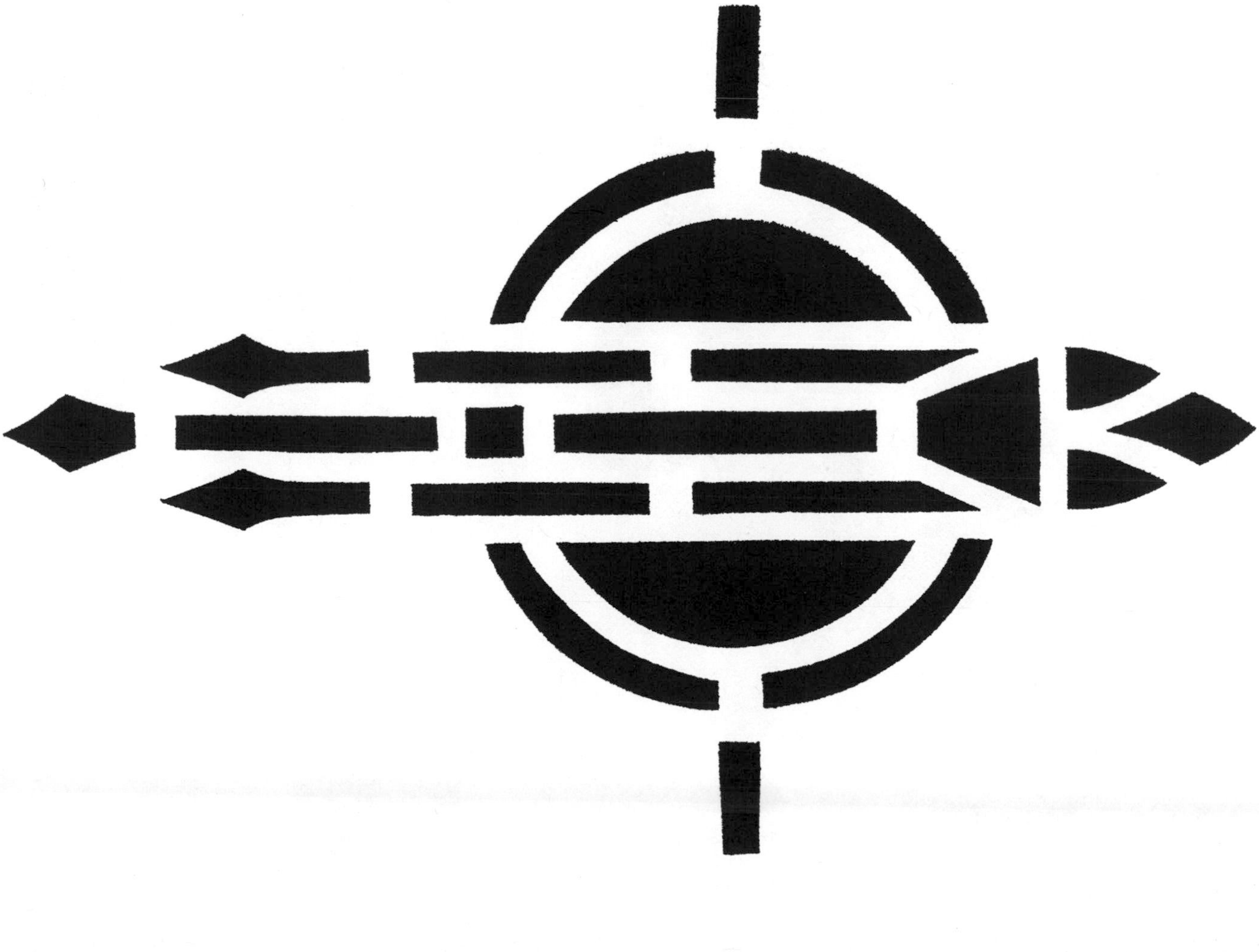

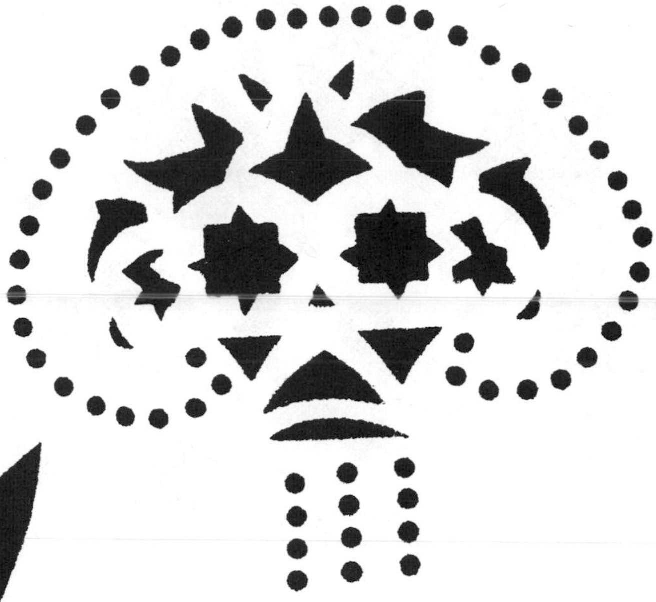

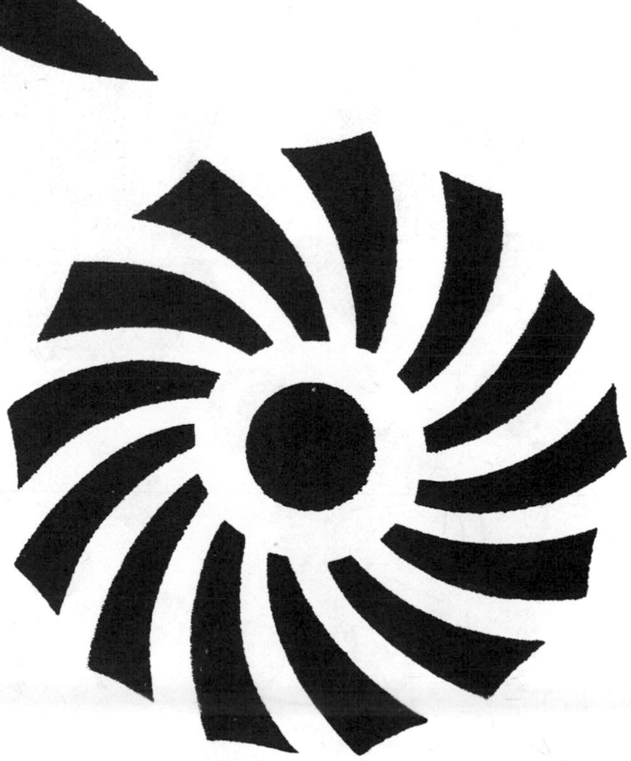

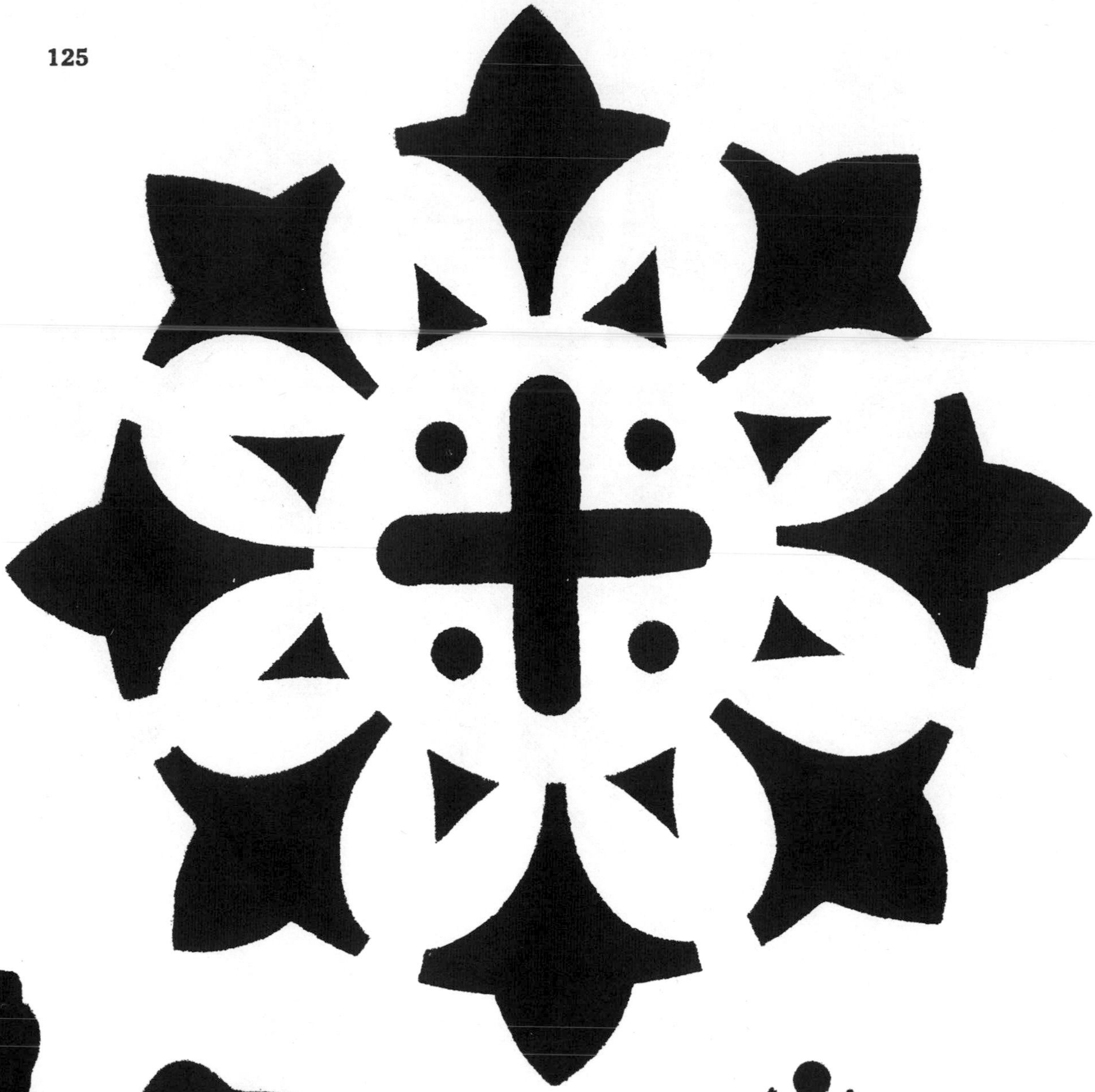

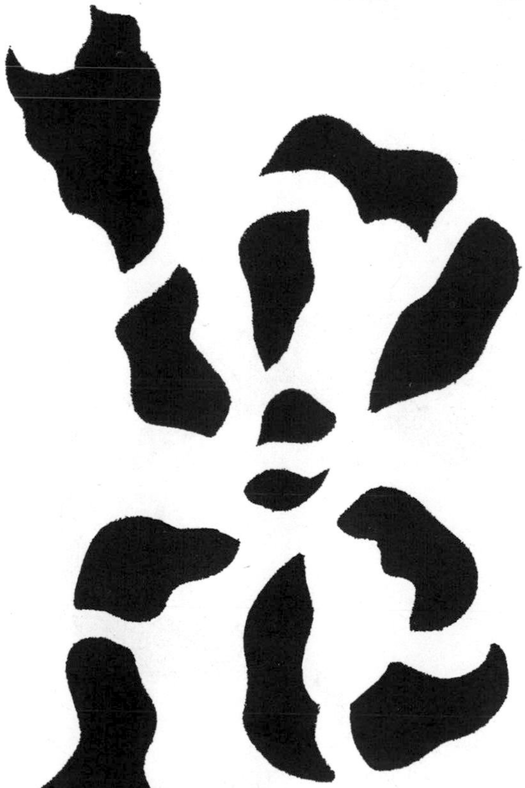

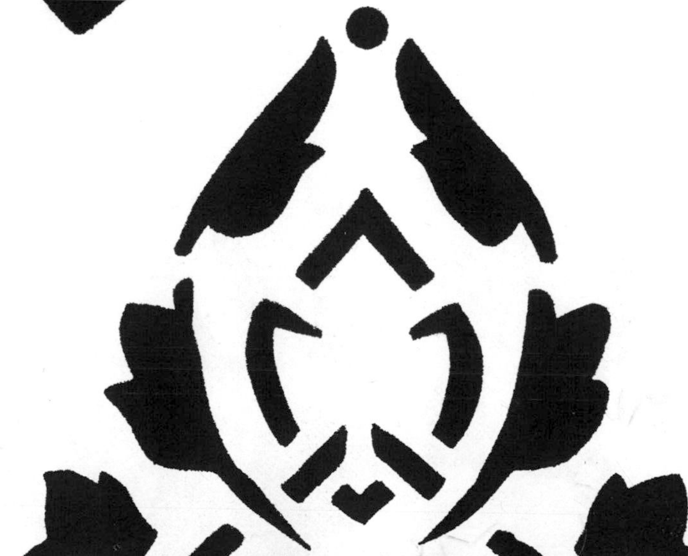

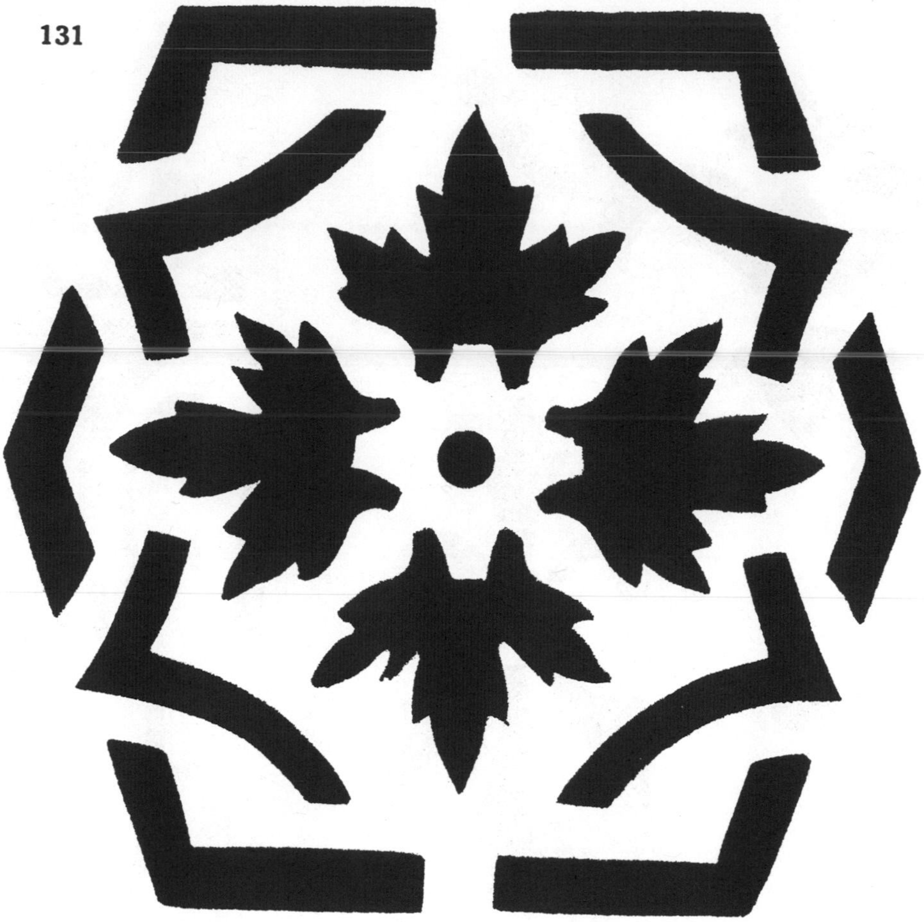

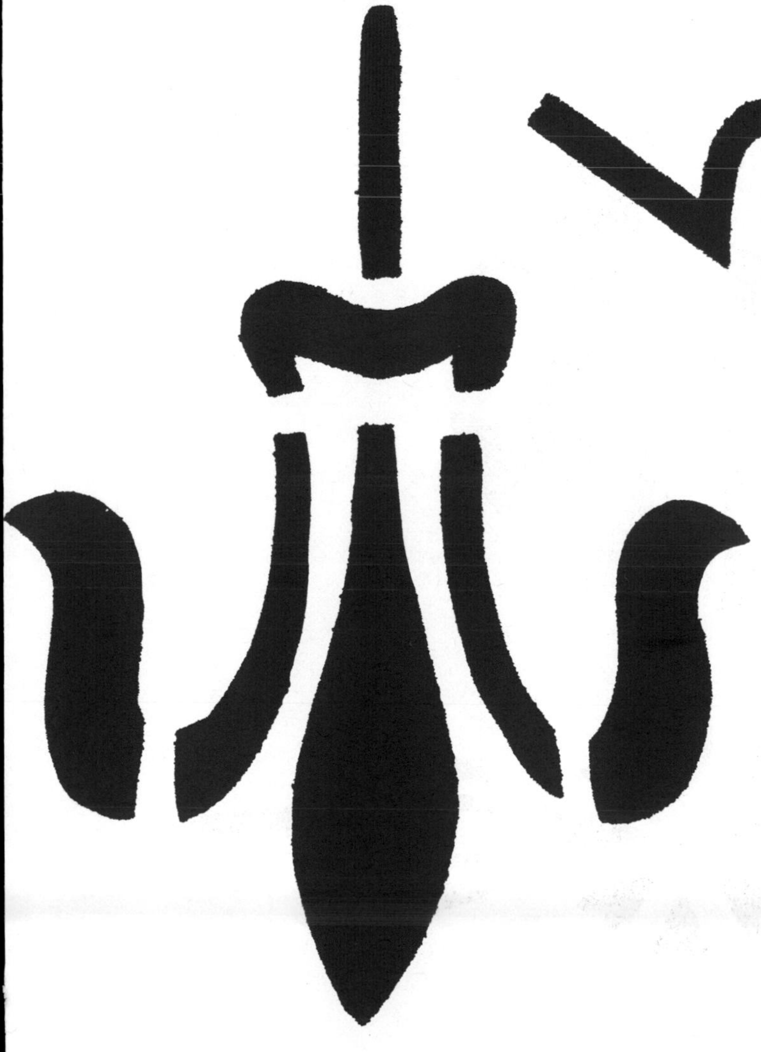

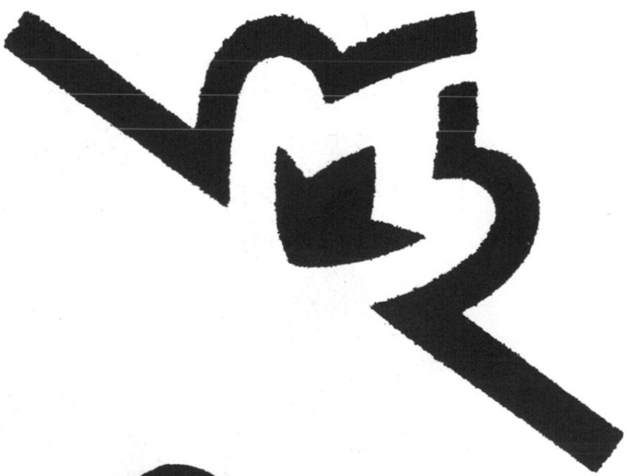

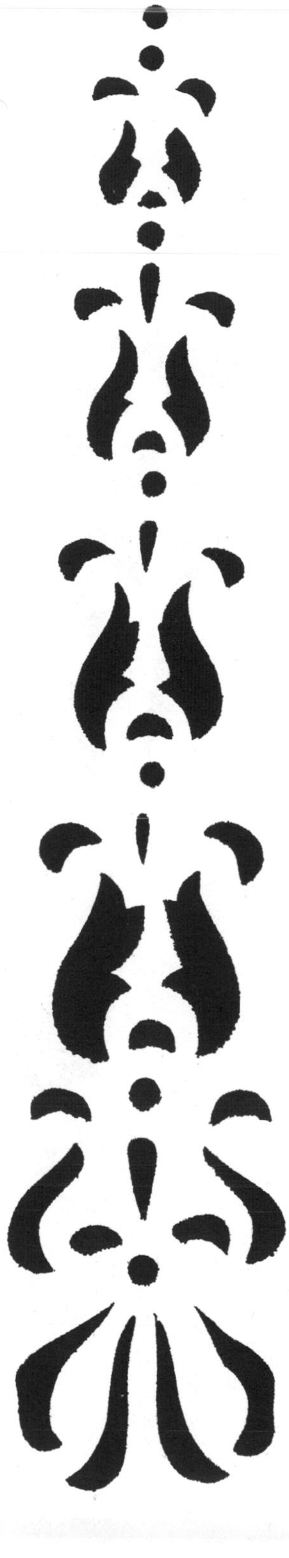

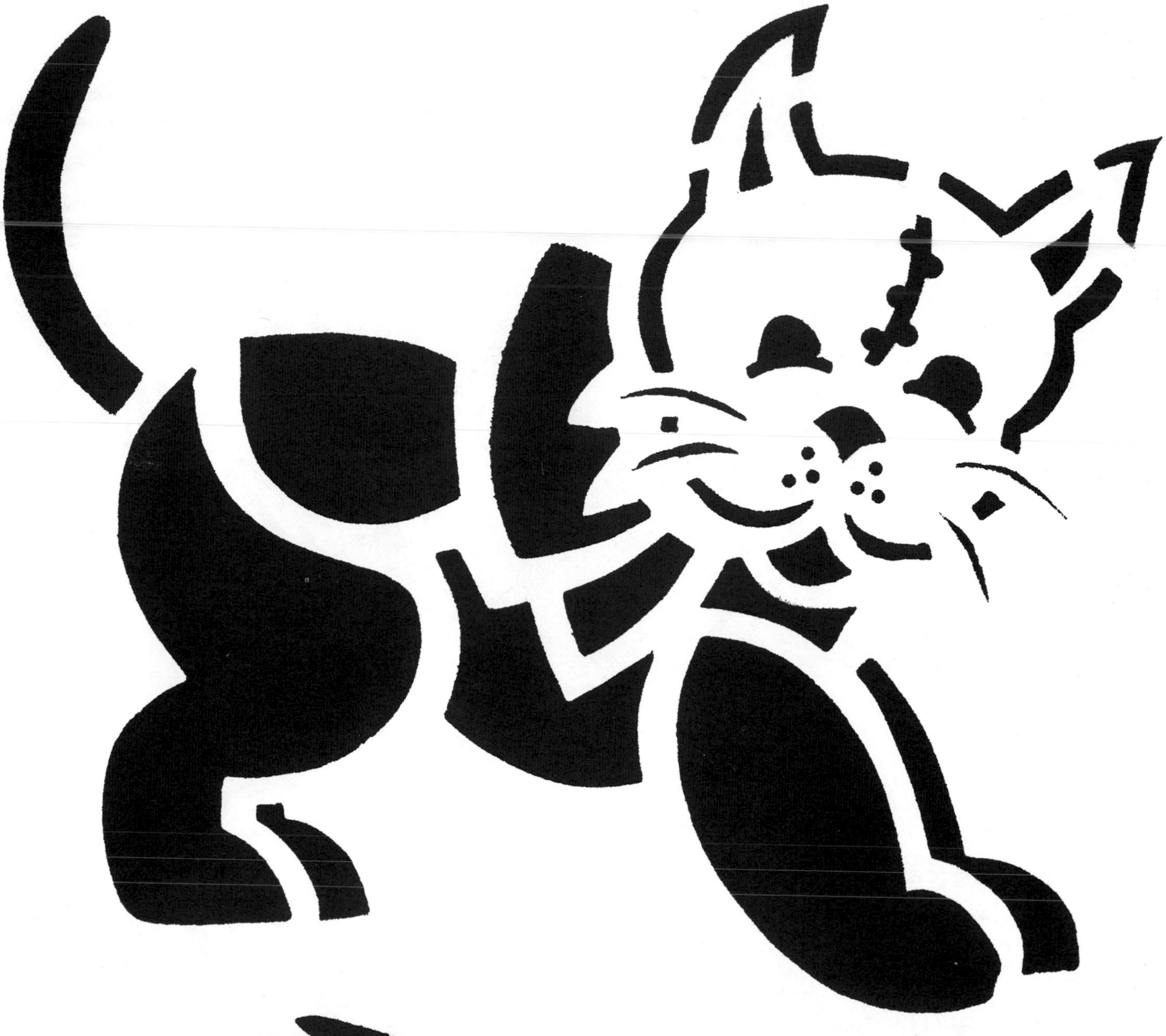

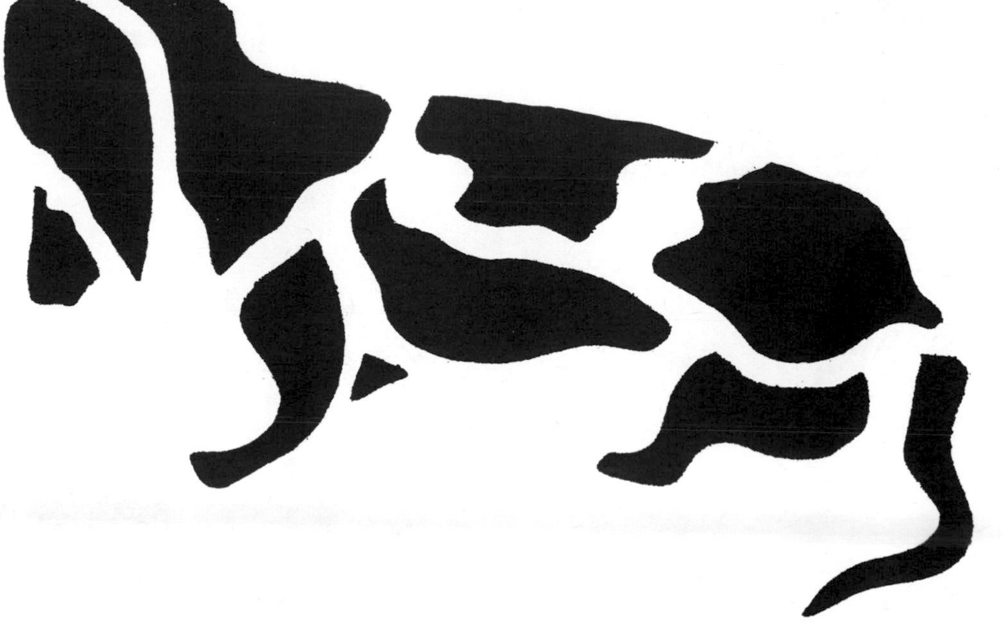

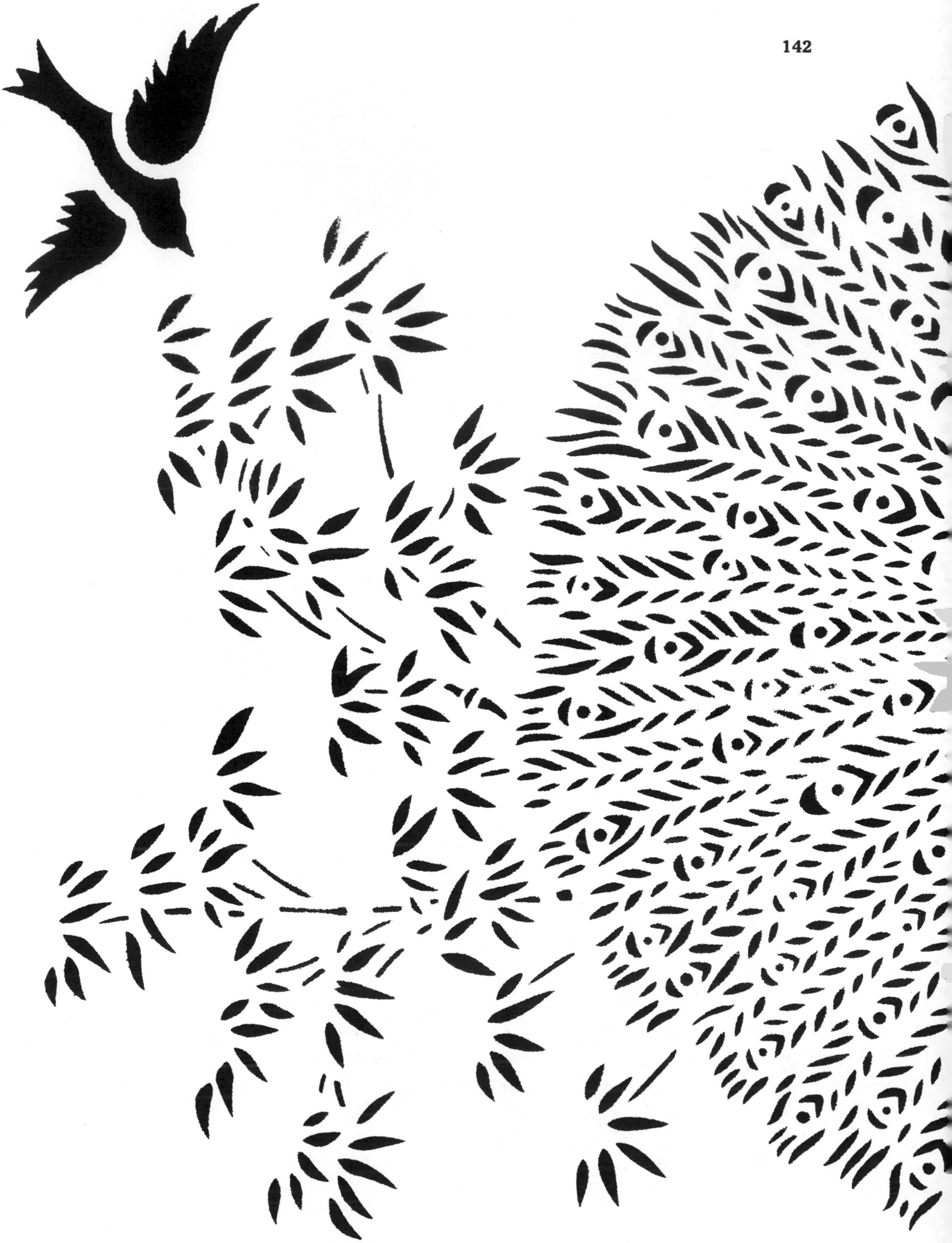

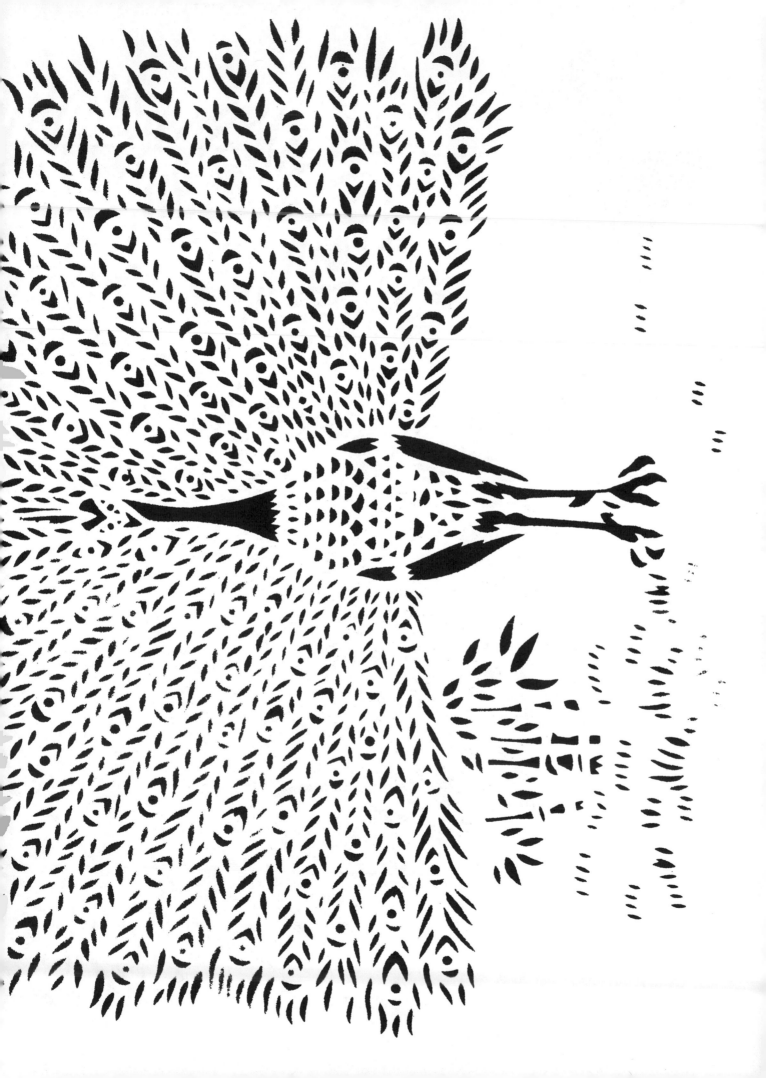

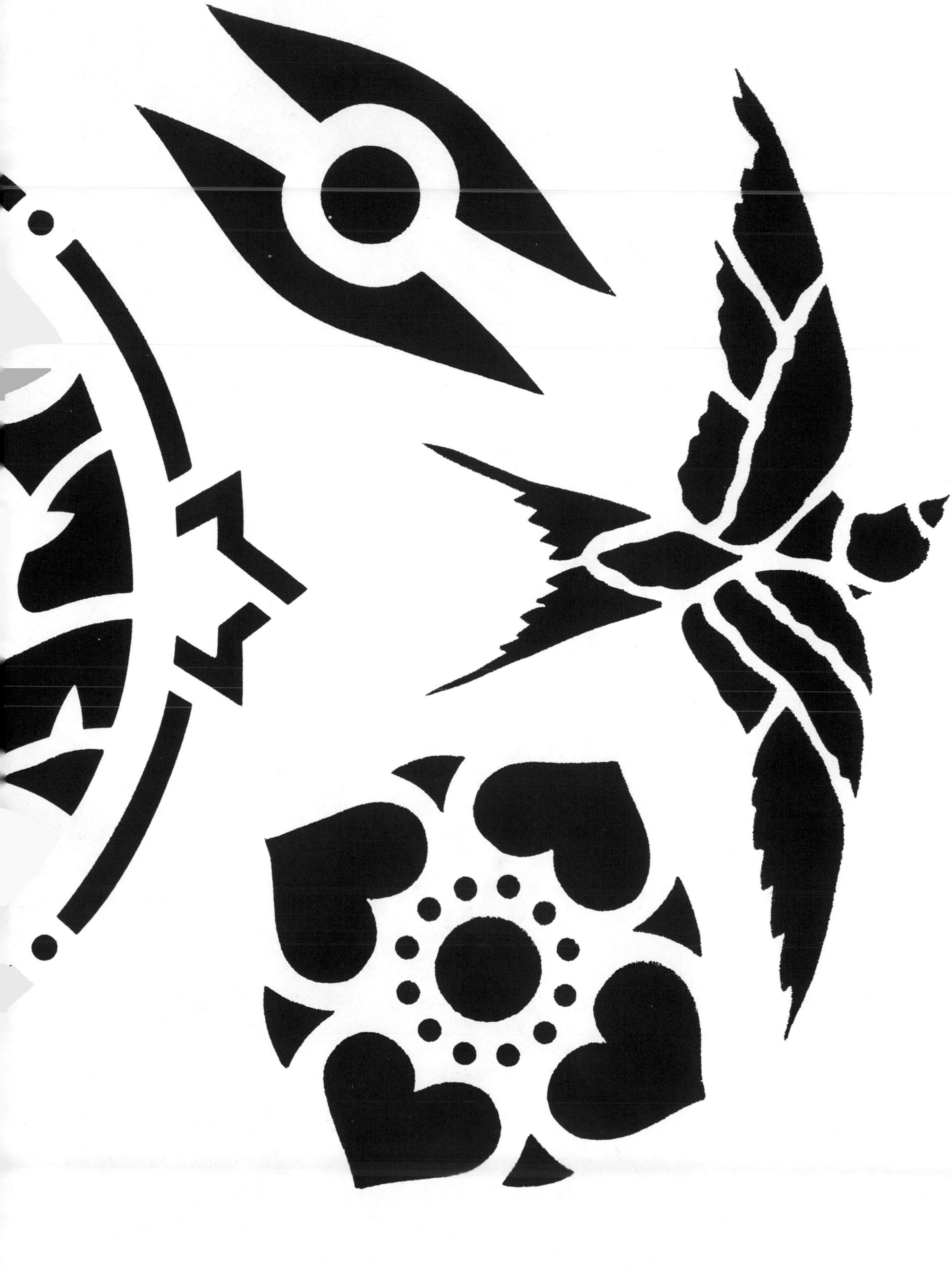

DIAPERS

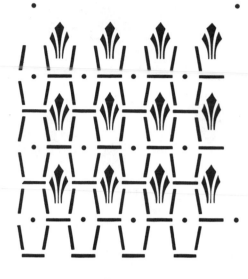

BORDERS

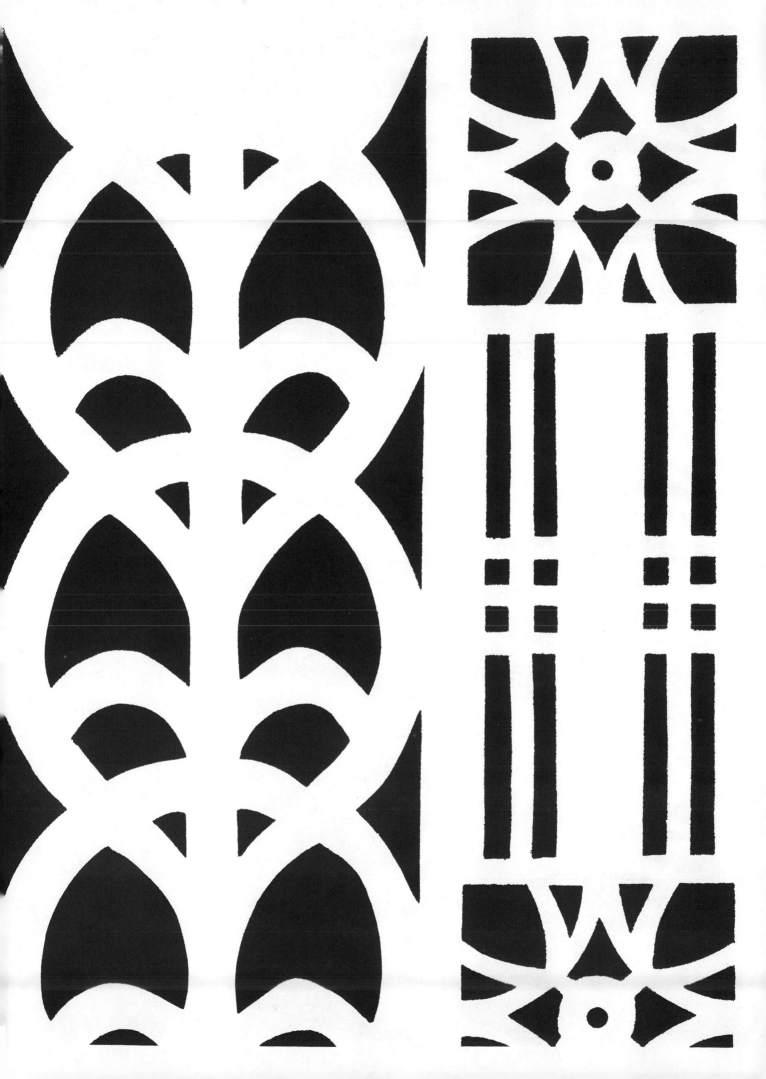

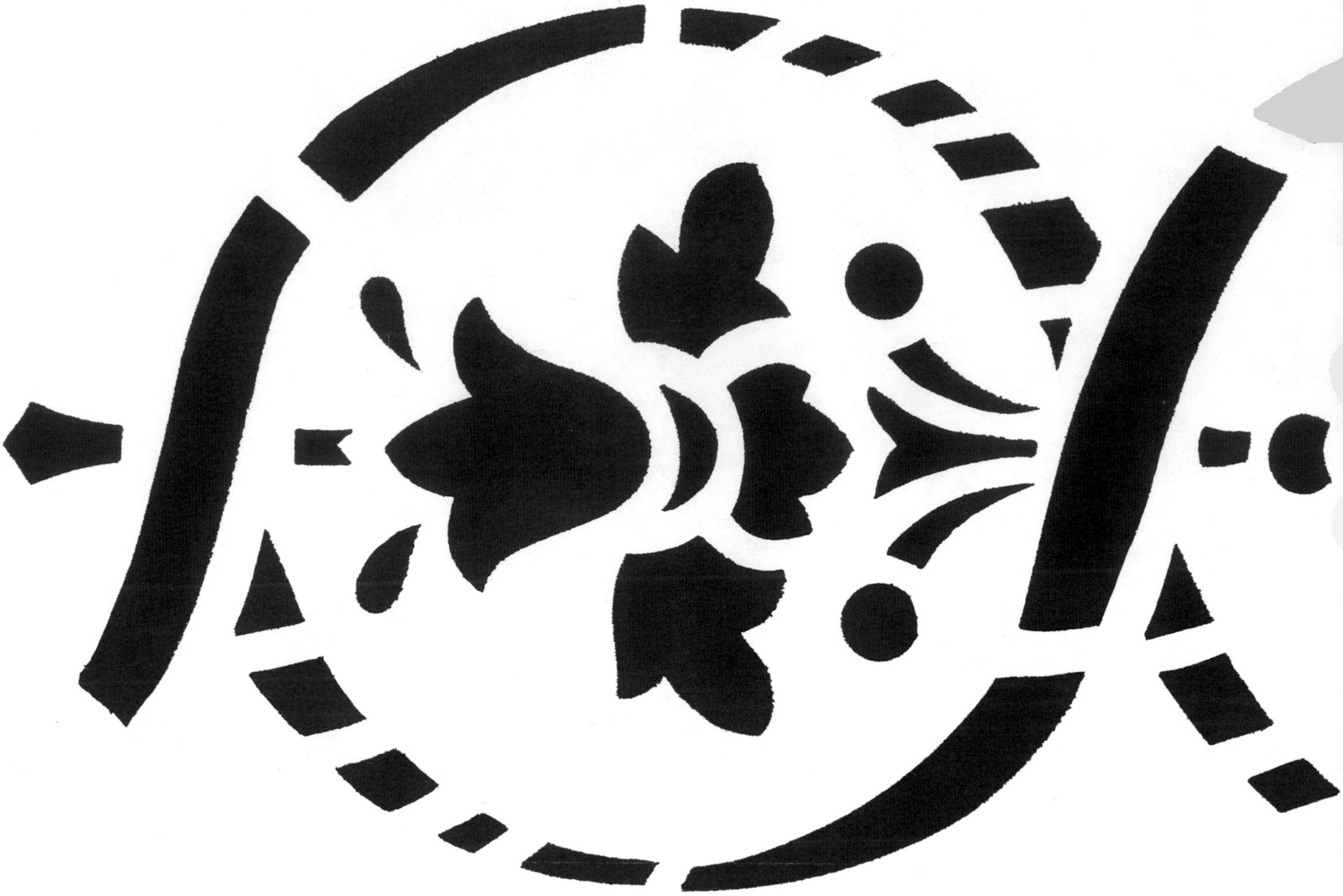

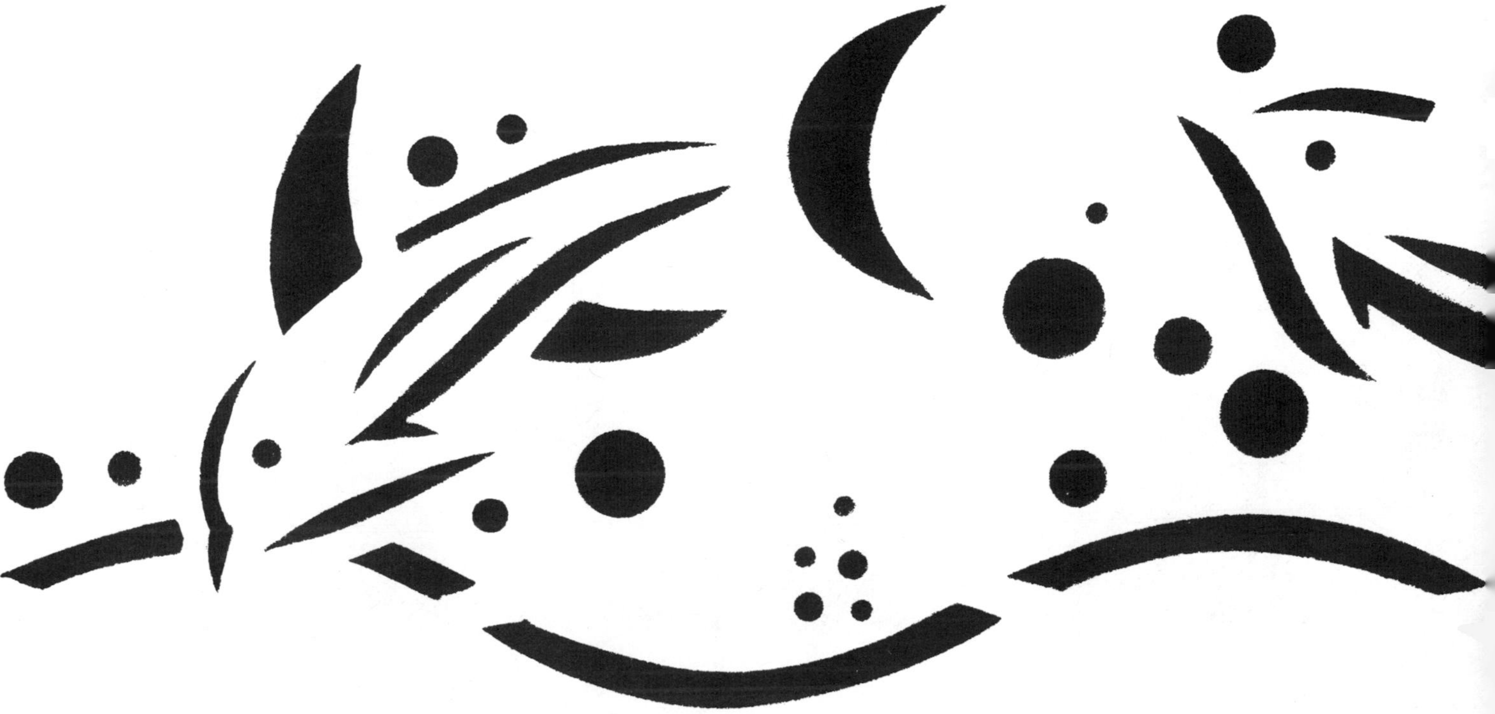

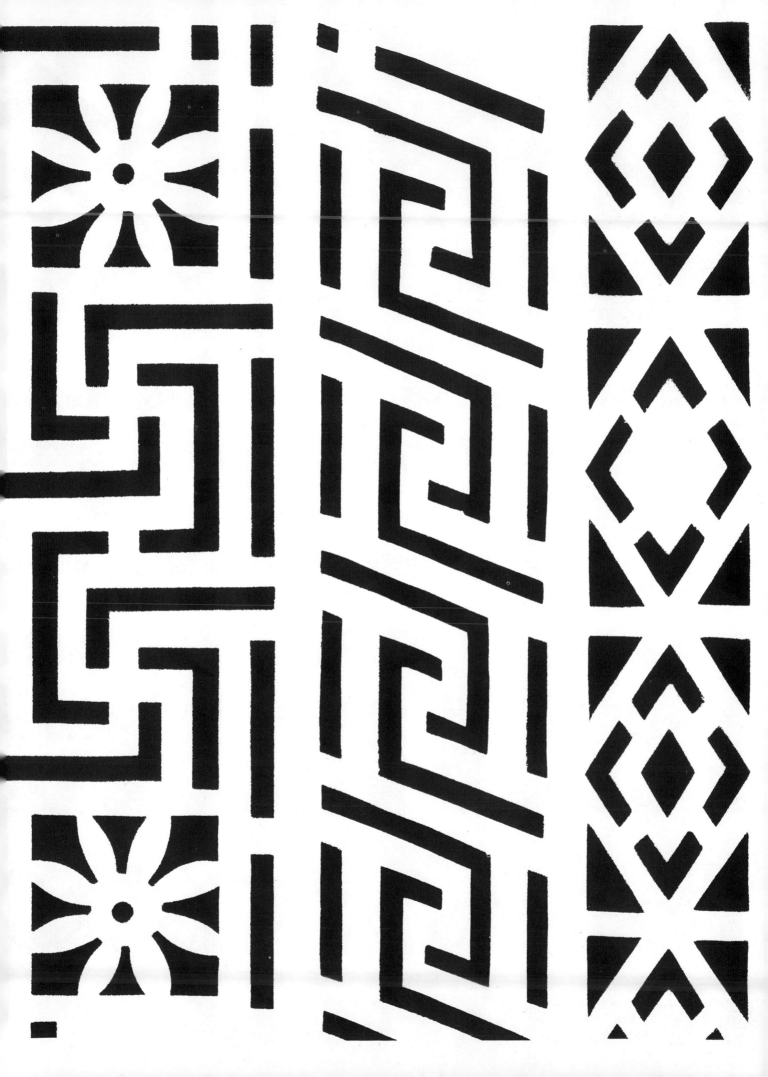

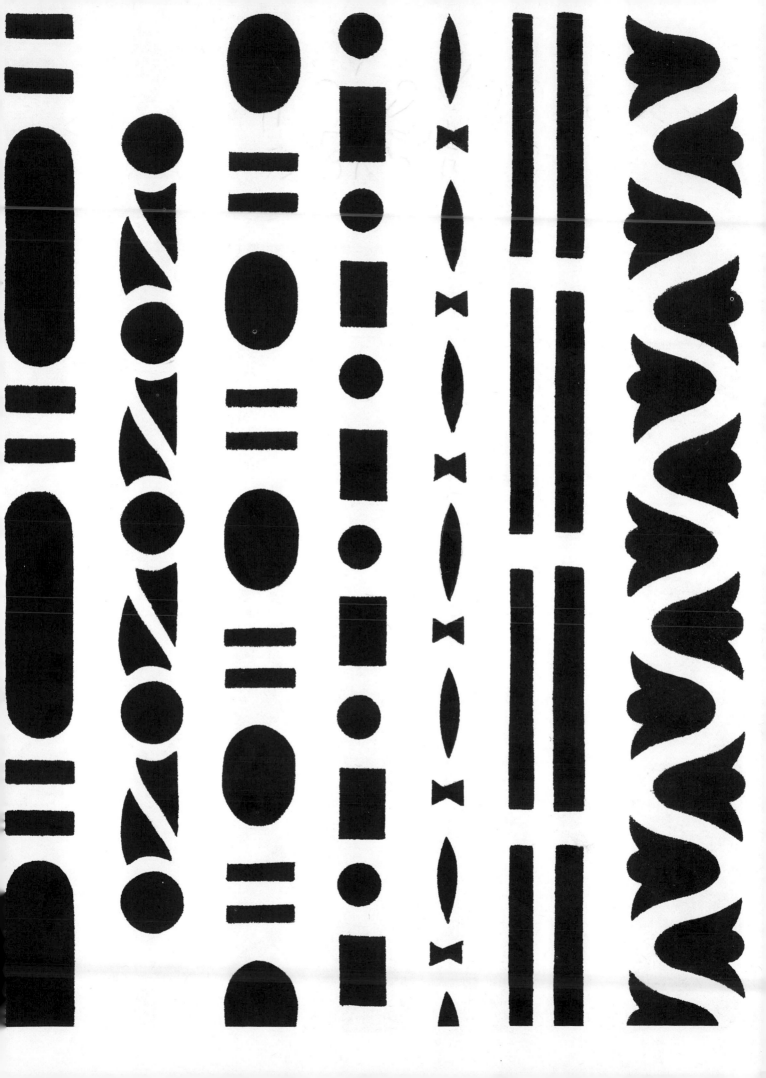

BIBLIOGRAPHY

Audsley, George Ashdown, and Berthold Audsley. *Artistic and Decorative Stenciling*. Boston, Massachusetts: Small, Maynard and Co., 1916.

Duthie, Arthur Louis. *Stencils and Stencilling for All Purposes; Artistic and Decorative*. The decorator series of practical handbooks, #10. London, England: Trade Papers Publishing Co., Ltd., 1914.

Glass, Frederick James. *Stencilcraft*. The artistic, practical handicraft series, #7. London, England: University of London Press, Ltd., 1927.

Scott-Mitchell, Frederick. *Practical Stencil Work*. The decorator series of practical handbooks, #2. London, England: Trade Papers Publishing Co., Ltd., 1906.

Smith, Frederick Richard. *Stencilling*. Pitman's craft-for-all series, #13. London, England: Sir I. Pitman & Sons, Ltd., 1930.

Sutherland, William George. *Stencilling for Craftsmen*. The Decorative Art Journal series, #4. Manchester, England: The Decorative Art Journals Co., Ltd., 1925.

Vanderwalker, Fred Norman. *New Stencils and Their Use*. Chicago, Illinois: F. J. Drake and Co., 1918.

INDEX